·T·FOGARTY

ADVENTURES IN UNDERSTANDING

"I usually prefer the little roads, the little, unexpected curving, leisurely country roads."

ADVENTURES
IN UNDERSTANDING

By

DAVID GRAYSON

Illustrated by

THOMAS FOGARTY

GROSSET & DUNLAP, *Publishers*

By arrangement with
Doubleday, Doran & Company, Inc.

CL

CONTENTS

INTRODUCTION

"A lute player," observes one of the wisest of the old philosophers, "when he is singing for himself, has no anxiety." So indeed it is with the writer. It is only when he is writing for himself that he writes happily.

Always since my youth I have loved to make notes in small books wherein I set forth the common adventures of my day, describe faithfully the people I meet when I take to the road, or report the interesting arguments I often have with them, in most of which, since I myself write them down afterward, I easily come out ahead. If I am sad I find comfort in setting down the nature of my sadness, for I come thus to a kind of philosophical understanding of it. If I am glad I turn with no less eagerness to my pen, for a joy expressed is a joy doubled. Thus I write away my sorrows and increase my joys. I challenge thus my doubts: thus define my aspirations. In all this writing I am without anxiety, for, like the lute player mentioned by Epictetus, I sing for myself.

When I consider making a new book, I look into these notes of mine and, having come upon an incident or an observation that sets me aglow with remembered enthusiasm, I say to myself, if it concerns a new friend, like the Iceman, "Now, wasn't that a man worth knowing!" Or if an experience like my adventures in Caliphry, "Who could have imagined anything more amusing?" Or if a bit of philosophy, I say, "It's true, it's true!" The more vividly these fine things come back to me, the more clearly it seems to me I understand what they mean, and the more I think I should like to share them with my friends. They seem somehow to count in making this a livable world. So I straightway warm up to my task and out of such "adventures in understanding," developed and rounded out, I make my book.

I suppose this is a wayward and unregenerate process of writing, but it seems to be the only way I know. Not long ago—while I was setting down the chapter herein called "Jonas" (over which I had much delight) I ran across a delicious passage in Benvenuto Cellini's Memoirs which has given me no end of comfort, since it encourages me in my perversity.

Cellini here relates the disgust and anger of King Francis because, when the King orders him to produce "twelve silver statues," he appears with a "salt cellar and a vase and busts," to say nothing of "a heap of other things that quite confound me."

"That," said I, gloating over the passage, "is just like me. I start out to produce twelve silver chapters—and see what common things I make. Salt cellars!"

"You have neglected my wishes," said King Francis to Cellini, "and worked for the fulfilment of your own."

What a sinner!

"If you stick to your own fancies," continued King Francis in what must have been a terrifying tone, "you will run your head against a stone wall."

"Here am I," said I, "with my head already against a stone wall."

So here is my book—common salt cellars,

vases that I have liked to make, busts without a torso or legs! Things that quite confound me when I consider them. But I have enjoyed writing every line of it. May you enjoy reading it.

DAVID GRAYSON.

ADVENTURES IN UNDERSTANDING

I

WE GO TO THE WICKED CITY

"Sail forth! Steer for the deep waters only!
For we are bound where mariner has not yet dared to go,
And we risk the ship, ourselves and all."

WHEN the Great War broke into my quiet
it changed all things for me. I am a
settled countryman and love well the hills of
Hempfield, where I live, and my own wide valley and the pleasant open fields; but in war you
do not do what you wish but what you must.

I had to live in a City—at first sadly enough
—and there I wrote laborious articles and
books. For it was not with a sword, nor yet

1

with a plough that I served, but with a pen.
That drudgery!

But at the same time I was living another
book—a high, free, true, adventurous book.
And this I have been writing down a little
at a time, as I could, for seven years. (It is
more than seven years since "Great Posses-
sions," more than seventeen since "Adventures
in Contentment.") I have called it from the
first "Adventures in Understanding," for it
seemed to me that in the City I came to understand many strange new things, both without and within, new things about life and
people, and the way to live.

I shall never forget the strange sense of adventure I had when we arrived at our chosen
lodging: the old doorway with the fanlight
over it and an aged wistaria vine tightly
twisted into the rusty iron railings.

"That," said I to Harriet, pointing to a tree
that looked hopefully around the corner from
the alley into the street, like a gossipy old
woman, "is a Tree of Heaven."

This old part of the city is full of such
ailanthus trees, which have a peculiar personality of their own. I came later to wonder at
them and somewhat to like them for the cheer-

ful way in which they accepted the hard fate of growing in back alleys, in the crevices of brick walls, or among paving-stones. But Harriet looked sceptical and seemed to doubt whether a true tree of heaven could be so much at home in a city.

Presently the door opened at the hand of the redoubtable Mrs. Jensen, who, I promise you, shall be much better known to you in the future.

The curious smell of living when the door opened; and the mystery of the long, narrow, dim stairway upward.

"Here we are," said I.

Harriet said nothing grimly, but I know as well what she was thinking as though she spoke aloud:

"Now, I wonder who lived here before, and whether they were nice, respectable, clean people."

The English language has one adequate word to express Harriet's approach to these complicated wonders: "Gingerly."

I have since looked up this excellent word in my dictionary:

"Gingerly: in a cautious, scrupulous, or fastidious manner."

And the quotation given to illustrate the word:

"*Gingerly,* and as if treading upon eggs, Cuddie began to ascend the well-known pass." Scott: *Old Mortality.* Vol. II, p. 53 (T. & F., 1867).

Since then, whenever I think of Harriet with her umbrella and armadillo basket mounting those wild, dark stairs to our chosen tower, I say to myself, under my breath:

"Gingerly, as if treading upon eggs, Cuddie began to ascend the well-known pass."

As for me, I liked, at once, the old street and the old house with the lichens of human living upon it; and the old rooms which were to be ours, and the wide court at the back with ailanthus trees in it and little fenced yards, and, here and there, on a clothes-line, a domestic tragedy. An old street, in an old, forgotten, neglected corner of the town! But I liked such places: old quiet places, places to look out of; old, still, sunny places, and beautiful people going by. I like to think of windows that have been much looked through; rooms full of thoughts left over out of life. There is a chill, inhuman cleanness about a new place; but something warm, familiar, pleasing in an old house. Here men have dreamed and women loved; here, possibly, one was born and one died. Here a fool meditated a selfish deed, thinking it would bring him happiness; and a wise man reflected upon the folly of taking anything for himself out of life that all other men could not also have for themselves upon the same terms (as Whitman says). Something, I scarcely know what, but it is real, seems to remain of all human contacts. Nothing human is ever wholly lost.

"But," said Harriet sensibly, "most people are so careless—so dirty!" (She thinks I have queer ideas.)

"Harriet," I replied, "I wish they weren't; but still I've got to have them. They're valuable. I can't get along without a single one of them, And," said I, "you remember what Henry James's artist replied to the critic who found so much dirt in Old Rome: 'What you call dirt,' said this artist, 'we call colour.' "

To this remark Harriet deigned no reply.

I may as well confess, first as last, that I found the early days of our life in the city not easy to bear. I used to find myself thinking of a little turning in the country road near the Hempfield creamery, where one catches the first clear view of the hills—I kept thinking of that particular turning and the smoke I could often see from our own chimney. I am a friendly man and love people who pass by. Often and often, in the country, have I stopped work in my field or orchard to beard a passing traveller in the road and "swop a lie with him," as we sometimes say. Your country traveller likes to be stopped and asked the price of apples or told about the condition of the weather (which he knows already).

But the people in the city streets: How they surged by entirely regardless of me! They did not seem to know that I was there. I was oppressed with populations, overcome with speed. It seemed to me that there was no place anywhere to be quiet or to think, no height from which I could look away to distant beautiful things.

Moreover, I found my labour heavy and difficult. A man should never write under compulsion: a man should write only when he is in love with somebody or something (as I am now). But in these days the Press was to me an inhuman monster, black with ink, roaring and ravening, pursuing me in a kind of nightmare race—pressing, pressing!—with me just escaping each week from being swallowed alive.

All this, added to the sense I had of a thundering Great War going on just around the corner (or so it seemed), made it appear for a time as if everything fine, simple, natural, beautiful in the world had shrivelled up and blown away.

So often the only way to get a man to look up is to get him down. A man utterly on his back has to look up. I remember one evening, after many days of dull labour, glancing out of the window near my table.

It was May, with a kind of softness in the air. The sun was going down, but still glowed upon the upper stories of the houses opposite. On an iron balcony I could see a child leaning to look over into the shadowy valley below. Men and women were here and there in the curious little boarded yards, working or talking.

Suddenly, something down deep within me seemed to come alive. I cannot rightly describe it; but all at once this scene, which had scarcely before awakened any reaction at all within me—unless it was aversion—became strangely and suddenly interesting, curious, human. I seemed to catch a harmony I had not heard before.

I leaned farther out.

The ailanthus trees were coming into leaf and held up to me their new green whorls— the peace offering of spring. I could hear pleasant confused voices without catching distinctly any words at all.

Presently a girl's voice from some nearby open window—though I could not see the girl herself—broke out singing:

"There are smiles——"

An instant later the half-mocking voice of a boy, from another window, joined in: "smiles that make you s-a-a-d"—and I heard the girl's voice trailing away in laughter.

All at once the oppression of the city, the oppression of too many people, left me. It seemed curiously and newly interesting to have all around me so many human beings, so much warm, strange, tragic, beautiful, brief human life.

I leaned still farther out.

Such a variety of odd activities! What were they all doing? What were they thinking about? Were they happy? Or miserable? What did they read? Had they any God? And, above all, why did they live all crowded together in such honeycombs of places, when there was room enough and to spare in the open country?

"How excited you look," said Harriet, when I turned to glance at her.

"Harriet," said I, "have you thought of all the extraordinary and interesting things that must be happening at this moment in these little pigeonholes of places, in these caverns and burrows and strange passageways?"

"No," said Harriet, "I have not."

"I think," said I, "that I have never before seen such a tangle of human life as there is right here under our eyes. I did not know it was here before. It seems to me I'd like to get down into it—all over."

It was then that I had the curious flashing vision (I'm going to confess everything!) of this room of mine at the dingy top of a city lodging house as a Tower. It improved it immediately. It was my Tower: and this was the City Wall I lived upon; high up, overlooking the world. It was something to live in a Tower on the Wall of the City, I would have you know. One could see much from a Tower!

"David," said Harriet, "what *are* you laughing at?"

"Do you remember, Harriet, when Nehemiah was rebuilding the wall of Jerusalem?"

"Yes," said Harriet.

"And how they got tired of seeing him perched up there and wanted him to come down among common human beings and be sociable?"

"Yes," said Harriet; "but—"

"And do you remember what Nehemiah said: 'I am doing a great work, so that I cannot come down.' "

When I said no more, Harriet asked presently, "What of it, David?"

"Well," said I, "it's extraordinary how many men think they are doing a Great Work and cannot come down."

"But Nehemiah *was* doing a great work," said Harriet.

"That," said I, "is different."

After that my nights and Sundays began to be much more cheerful. I began to go all about our neighbourhood, first, like a careful explorer, near shore, but little by little I ventured into deeper waters and sailed by unknown countries. And I began to look upon these shores for some native I could pounce upon, like a kind of good-humoured pirate, and carry off captive to my Tower. It seemed to me that there must be a way, if one could find it, of getting to these strange people.

When once we come to this mood, adventure is never far in the offing, and comes upon us in the most surprising ways.

If any one had told me that I should stumble upon my first adventure at the foot of my own Tower, I should surely not have believed it—but so it was. For adventure is like love—we do not have to seek far for it; we can begin anywhere. I think sometimes we mistake the nature both of love and of adventure; and sit by waiting for someone else to begin the loving, or for some fine and thrilling thing to happen to us. But true love is not like that—nor yet beautiful adventure. Love comes of loving first, and adventure, because we have it in the soul of us.

I had come down the stairs at evening and stood looking up the street. In the block above, an Italian was playing on a street organ. Rendered soft by the distance, it was somehow sweet to hear. An evening breeze off the harbour, with a touch of salt in it, came cheerfully in at one end of the street and went out at the other. I had to admit, grudgingly, that the city, after all, had a kind of beauty of its own.

Presently my eye lighted upon the substantial figure of Mrs. Jensen, standing below me in the little front area-way that led into her basement burrow. She had her hands folded upon her capacious apron and was looking out for a moment in the cool of the evening, benevolently, upon the passing world.

"Good-evening, Mrs. Jensen," said I.

"Good-evening," said she.

I think I profit by looking something like a farmer.

"Did you ever live in the country, Mrs. Jensen?" I asked.

"No," said she.

"Never had any hens, or pigs, or bees?"

"No," said she.

"Never made a garden?"

"No," said she; "but Jensen, he's crazy about gardens. Jensen, he makes gardens in the house."

She spoke in a rather guttural voice, with a slight foreign inflection.

"Does he? What kind of a garden? Right here in the city?"

"Sure," said Mrs. Jensen broadly. "Sure. Every year he has flowers, and sometimes vegetables. Oh, not many, but good. This year the vegetable he is planting is punkin."

"But how can he do it?" said I, in astonishment.

"How can any one make a garden among all these stones?"

When Mrs. Jensen laughs she shakes in the middle. I could see I had her interested, and presently she was leading me down the steps and through a dark passageway to a large room at the back of the house.

"Jensen," said she, "here's Mr. Grayson, and he wants to see how you plant vegetables."

At this I saw a man, who had been stooping over at work near the window, rise up and face me. He was a slight man with greying hair thrust back in disorder. He looked a little like pictures I have seen of Beethoven. A fine, sensitive, serene face, upon which was written as it were in capital letters, "Impractical." But I liked him at once.

Jensen smiled deprecatingly at this bold introduction. I could see that he was embarrassed.

"I'm from the country," said I, "and I like to see things grow. I was surprised to hear about your flowers—"

"And vegetables," put in Mrs. Jensen.

"Oh, it is nothing," said he.

He said "iss nutting," for he had still more of the foreign burr in his voice than his wife. He was a Dane.

At that I discovered that the whole back window was full of bloom. On little shelves cunningly constructed close to the glass were many pots containing daffodils, narcissus, and tulips, now coming into full blossom and filling the air with as rare a fragrance as ever in the country.

"How fine your flowers are!" I exclaimed.

"It iss nutting!" And he spread out his hand apologetically.

"He makes nutting of ever'ting," remarked Mrs. Jensen.

"We have not here enough sunlight," he said. "They grow veak. It iss not like the country."

But they gave true evidence of much loving care. I know well the sign of the man who loves growing things: how his hands touch them gently. It took no time at all to warm him into enthusiasm. His face began to flush and a light came into his eyes. He told me of each variety and even the peculiarities of each plant, the obstinacy of this one, the enterprise of that one, how this one was tricky and that thirsty.

"But where is your vegetable garden?" I asked presently.

"This year," remarked Mrs. Jensen, "the vegetable he is planting is punkin."

Jensen led me out of the door into the little pocket-handkerchief of a stone court. I did not see so much as a square foot of garden space.

"There," said he with pride.

Close to the wall stood a large wooden box filled with earth. Jensen told me how he had brought in this earth pail by pail from a distant lot, and how he had gathered manure from the street outside; he showed me the cunning device he had invented for sprinkling his garden by way of a bit of hose from the kitchen tap just within the window. All around the edges of his box he had radishes and lettuce, already growing quite thriftily, and in each corner, with mathematical precision, he had set a cabbage plant; but what he especially pointed out was the new adventure of the year—pumpkins—which were just thrusting their bent green knees out of the moist earth. Jensen tenderly flecked away a bit of earth here and there as if to help them in their struggle to emerge.

"Jensen, he likes vegetables," said Mrs. Jensen.

"But where in the world," I asked, thinking of the activities of a really energetic pumpkin vine, "are they to run to?"

This caused Jensen to laugh aloud, and with the greatest triumph. His face literally glowed.

"It iss so in the city," said he, "that there iss not room to grow out, so ve grow up!"

He illustrated this process vividly with both head and arms.

"So vit men, so vit punkins."

I saw then that here was a philosopher as well as a gardener—though I knew beforehand that all true gardeners become, sooner or later, philosophers.

Jensen showed me with delight a little trellis he was then building on the brick wall leading upward.

"Ve haf plenty room," said he, chuckling; "ve can go up to the sky!"

I had a vision of great yellow pumpkins adorning the side of the house all the way up, which was altogether so amusing that I couldn't help laughing.

"But when the pumpkins get large," I asked, "how are you going to keep them from breaking away or pulling the vines down?"

I wish you could have seen Jensen at that moment—tapping his head with two fingers, his eyes twinkling, saying mysteriously:

"I haf a great idea,"—but refusing to tell me what it was.

At this I glanced at Mrs. Jensen. There she stood, shaking her head slowly from side to side and saying:

"Jensen, he lofes vegetables."

But the wonders had only begun. Jensen now exhibited another box, much smaller, so that it could be carried in, if necessary. He did not need to show me what it contained, for no sooner did he open the grated lid than I had olfactory information! Rabbits. He pointed out the pair and observed:

"There will be more soon," which I did not doubt.

From this we went inside, and I made the acquaintance of his sleepy canary birds, each in a cage of its own, for which Jensen had made curtains to keep out the evening light. There

were also a bowl of goldfish and a cat. He
came so near having a complete menagerie that
I asked finally in my soberest voice:

"Where's the pony?"

They both looked at me in solemn surprise.
Jensen recovered first.

"Ach, you are a joker." Only he said,
"yoker."

Mrs. Jensen here put in, as though somehow
to answer a reasonable question.

"Jonas, he hass a flivver."

Jonas, I learned, was their son. I had no
premonition then of what possibilities and ex-
citements were wrapped up in the "flivver" of
Jonas. That is another epic.

I cannot tell what delight I took in all these
simple discoveries. I suppose they could have
been duplicated in a thousand cramped yards
and area-ways in that great city, but they were
new to me. And it seemed to me, in the
warmth of my enthusiasm, that here, in this
dim basement, was a kind of ideal life—nature
indeed balked, but human nature somehow triumphant under handicaps. Here were people
who managed to live interestingly. But it is
a strange thing that people who get the credit
of living ideal lives often do not see it in that

light at all. No sooner did I try to express something of my feeling than I unloosened the floods.

"Ah," said Mrs. Jensen, in her guttural voice, "ve have great troubles."

I looked at Jensen; the glow was dying out of his face. He was beginning to be uncomfortable, for he plainly knew what was coming. A moment before he had been the master, exhibiting his triumphs, and Mrs. Jensen was the worshipful follower, hanging breathless upon his words; but now she turned upon him suddenly, with a kind of indignation:

"Jensen, he can't get vork. He try and try, and he cannot get vork."

Jensen hung his head but said nothing.

"He iss no good, Jensen: he iss afraid of ever't'ing. He goes to ask for vork, and when the boss says 'No,' Jensen goes avay. He should not go avay. He should ask, 'Why?' Iss there not vork in America? Do not Americans have books to bind?"

By this time she had become vehement and glared fiercely upon poor Jensen, who seemed more and more to shrink into his unworthiness. Yes, he looked like some dreamy Beethoven. . . .

"So Mr. Jensen is a bookbinder," I said, to relieve the situation.

"He iss too much an artist for America. All they say in America is 'Qvick, qvick.' They do not want good vork, only qvick, qvick vork. And Jensen, he iss not qvick!"

And then, the hopelessness of the situation overcoming her, she seemed fairly to swell up in her indignation:

"Jensen, he vill not try qvickness. I tell him he live in America he must be qvick. But he say, 'I cannot be qvick.' Sooch a man!"

"I wonder," I said, "if any real artist is ever quick." But my remark made no impression whatever. She shook her head in complete helplessness.

"Ah, ve have such troubles. Food it costs so much and the rent is so high. And Jonas, he must have his flivver. Ah! ve have troubles."

Poor Jensen. He stood with hanging head, saying never a word. It was evidently an old experience with him.

"Well," I said, "I am interested in books. What kind of books do you bind?"

At this Mrs. Jensen started up with alacrity. "I vill show you," said she.

So she went to a drawer in a kind of dresser

and took out a parcel carefully wrapped in paper. This she unrolled and took out a leather-covered box beautifully fitted together. Opening this with hands as tender as those of a mother, she drew out a book. Jensen stood still, hanging his head, and did not look up. Mrs. Jensen handed the book to me with every solicitude. I thought it at the moment truly the most beautiful thing of the kind I had ever seen, rich green morocco, hand tooled in red and gold; all exquisitely perfect.

"What a beautiful piece of work!" I exclaimed.

I saw Jensen's head slowly rising. I looked at the book more closely.

"How perfectly your satin inner covers match the morocco!" I said.

At this Jensen took a step toward me and half lifted his hands.

"And where did you get such a design for the lettering? It's wonderful!"

"Ah! So you like it!" said Jensen.

I wish you could have seen the change in the man; from deepest dejection all in a moment to pride and power. He thrust one hand through his hair as though he were about to sit down and play a sonata. Then he took the book from me, and with a touch of loving tenderness, turned it over and over in his hands; showed me each difficult excellence, the tooling, the lettering, the pasting, the pressing. His face was glowing again and his eyes shining. His whole aspect became one of masterly dignity and pride. At the same time Mrs. Jensen seemed to fade away or shrink down again into her former place as worshipful admirer. It was as good as a play. She stood by, occasionally remarking, in her guttural voice, and with unmistakable pride:

"Ah, Jensen, he iss an artist!"

Then she would pause a moment, as though struggling with herself, and add, shrugging, "But he iss not qvick."

Suddenly Jensen turned to me with a look of affectionate confidence, like a child:

"So you are interested in books."

"Yes," said I, "I like the outsides of books when they are like this: I like still better the insides of books."

He had told me that this was a book he had just finished binding for a rich book-lover. It was an exquisite edition of the "Odes of Horace." I opened it almost at random and came across the ode to Mæcenas, inviting him

to the Sabine farm (which long ago I knew **well**), and I read aloud:

"Lord of himself that man will be,
And happy in his life alway,
Who still at even can say with free
Contented soul: 'I've lived to-day!'"

When I had finished, I was surprised to find Jensen taking hold of my hand with both of his—in quite an old-world way—and, after shaking it heartily, saying:

"Ah, ve know, ve know."

How I love to be accepted as a member of the Craft!

We had much more good and friendly conversation. I could hardly get myself away from these interesting people; and finally proposed that the Jensens come up some evening soon to see Harriet and me.

"There are plenty of questions in the world yet to be solved," said I. "You and I must get at them at once. They must be settled."

"Ve vill, ve vill," cried out Jensen, as I went up the stairs.

I heard the door shut behind me and then open suddenly, and Jensen's voice, full of enthusiasm:

"Ve've lived to-day!"

"We have," said I.

Then I heard Mrs. Jensen:

"Jensen, he iss an artist—but he iss not qvick"—and the door closed for good and all.

I came back to find Harriet much alarmed—thinking me lost in a strange city.

"Wherever have you been?" she asked.

"I have been out in society," said I. "Harriet, I've met an artist, a true gardener, and a philosopher."

"Who is he?" she asked.

This had not at all occurred to me before, and I said:

"Well, he's the husband of Mrs. Jensen——"

As I dropped off to sleep that night I said to myself:

"What a day! What a day! I could never have imagined it would be like this. It's no credit to a man in the country to have a garden; any one can have it and mishandle it in the country. But think of loving gardens so much as to make one among these stone caverns!"

I thought again of yellow pumpkins hanging to a brick wall, and went to sleep laughing.

II

I ADVENTURE INCOGNITO

A countryman may travel from kingdom to kingdom, province to province, city to city, and glut his eyes with delightful objects, hawk, hunt, and use these ordinary disports, without any notice taken, all of which a prince or a great man cannot do.—*The Anatomy of Melancholy.*

I WONDER if ever you change human beings with arguments alone: either by peppering them with little sharp facts or by blowing them up with great guns of truth. You scare 'em, but do you change 'em? I wonder if ever you make any real difference in human beings without understanding them and loving them. For when you argue with a man (how much more with a woman), you are somehow trying to pull him down and make him less (and yourself more); but when you try to understand him, when you like him, how eager is he then to know the truth you have; and you add to him in some strange way, you make him more than he was before; and at the same time, and that is the sheer magic of it, you yourself become more.

There is nothing in this world that people so much thrive upon, grow fine and rosy and robust upon (especially women) as being loved. This is true.

Yet there must be facts, and reasons, and arguments. . . .

How I toiled those long spring days in the City, forging thunderbolts of argument, heaping up ammunition of fact, loading great shells of truth.   Oh, I was hot upon the business of bringing down the enemy!   I'd finish 'em off! Once they heard the machine-gun rattle of *those* facts, or saw *that* bomb burst white in the sky, they'd run to cover!   Every day I grew savager and savager.

(Now, facts are not to be thrown at people like dishes or vegetables, but somehow warmed into them.)

But, thank God, I had my blessed nights and Sundays; and as soon as I began to look

up and look around, I began, as surely, to come
alive again. One Saturday morning I said to
Harriet, "I'm going to stop work early to-day
and take in the City."

Harriet, by her look—oh, I know Harriet!—
seemed to imply that I'd better look out lest I
be the one taken in; but, nevertheless, I set out
full of curiosity and enthusiasm.

I shall never forget that vivid spring morning. I walked briskly down the street, looking
all about me.

It was May in the City, and where is May
not beautiful? The vines were coming freshly
green on old walls, the elms were showing their
new soft verdure, the little squares of lawn here
and there by the street-side blessed the eye;
and in many a friendly window I could see the
beckoning welcome of potted daffodils or
narcissus.

"The City also," I said, "is very beautiful."

I looked in at curious alleys and openings as
I passed, and old area-ways and strange nooks
and corners. I love such irregularities, unexpected passageways, unopened but inviting
doorways; the odd shifts of human beings to
meet the small difficulties of life.

Presently, as I walked, I began to have a

strong sense, among all these hurrying people of the streets, of being utterly alone, aloof. It was as though I were wearing a magic cloak of invisibility, for it seemed that I could see all these passing people without their seeing me. They went by as though I were not there at all, had no corporeal existence. I became a kind of ghost, and quite depressed, there in the bright May sunshine—and yet felt that I was well worth knowing, if only someone would stop long enough to know me!

I paused on a busy corner to consider this curious problem.

"After all," said I, "I don't think I am really invisible. I am merely visiting the City incognito. I'm a kind of Caliph of democracy, arrived here from my palace in the country to visit, secretly, the humming streets of Bagdad."

This idea seemed to me so amusing that it ran away at once with my fancy. Ever since I was a boy, no story has interested me more than that of the Prince who goes out disguised among common people for a day of true happiness or a night of thrilling adventure. How all the ripe old Caliphs loved such doings!

And, when you come to think of it, is not this about the most ancient and universal of the stories known to man? It began at the very beginning!

It was only a short time after this earth was created—according to the veracious record— that the Lord God himself, no doubt grown lonesome, as royalty must, upon his high throne, came down in the cool of the day to walk in Eden. And what an adventure he had; and what goings-on among the inhabitants! At that time the entire population of the earth had just discovered that it was naked, and had organised the first great industry— garment-making. What a thing was that to find—offhand—by a Monarch travelling incognito!

"But in these latter days," said I, standing there in an eddy of the city stream, "royalty is not what it once was. It has grown unadventurous and blasé. It is willing to take its thrills second hand. It lacks fresh imagination. It has quite lost the genius of wonder. We are all of us kings nowadays, in cities at least, with ballots of folded paper for our sceptres; but we are so unsteady on our thrones, so little

certain of our royalty, that we dare not, even
for a moment, trust ourselves down among
ordinary, interesting Adams and Eves."

I liked this idea tremendously and quite forgot where I was in pursuit of it.

"No," said I, "the modern Caliph of democracy seems to fear that if he gets off his
throne and goes down among all these Italians,
Poles, Greeks, Jews, Negroes, he will not be
able to get back again. He wants to feel his
crown always warmly on his head—one hundred per cent on his head, as you might say. I
suspect he wears it at night, perhaps ties it
on with a pocket-handkerchief lest it fall off
and get lost under the bed. I think the real
trouble is that he does not feel, inside, quite
royally democratic."

So I walked onward again, but now with a
new and delightful idea, thinking myself truly
a kind of Caliph come all unknown to visit busy
Bagdad: "glutting his eyes with delightful
objects." And being a Caliph disguised, of
course these hurrying people would never
recognise me. I must therefore make the ad-
vances myself, find out the heroes and the
villains, and surprise adventure where she
lurked. Afterward, at my royal pleasure, I

could choose whether or not to disclose my
identity.

(Did you ever take flight upon the wings of a
wholly amusing and beguiling idea? Recklessly? Try it one day, friend, and be happy!)

By this time I had drifted well down toward
the wharves of the city and was looking sharply
at each man and woman I met, considering
where I should begin.

"Someone," said I, "though he doesn't know
it yet, is shortly to have a curious adventure."

But they kept rolling past me so fast that I
could not seem to fix upon any particular
person.

"The very next man," I said at last, "that I
find standing still I will swoop down upon."

Hardly had I formed this grand resolution
when, almost at my elbow, in the door of a little
cubby of a street shop, stood a stout, swart man
with black eyes and an inviting manner.

"Good-morning," said I promptly, recalling
my decision.

"Good-morning," he answered, and at once
backed into his shop and with a wave of his
hand motioned me to one of his tall chairs.

He was a bootblack.

I certainly wanted no shine; but I climbed

meekly into his chair, chuckling a little at myself because, after all my grand ideas of capturing some interesting human being, I had myself
been caught in one of the oldest nets in the
world and would presently have to pay the ran-
som of a dime to escape. . . . I was glad Harriet was not there.

The swart man went at his work with a will;
and presently, watching his head bent down before me, my fancy went free again, and I said
to myself:

"He evidently recognised my royalty by in-
stinct.   Has he not mounted me here, at once,
upon a throne?   Is he not making all these low
obeisances to me?   It's wonderful to be a
Caliph."

It was a stuffy little hole of a place, no larger
than a Hempfield hen coop, with four chairs in
a row, a kerosene stove in one corner, and
brightly coloured pictures of the King and
Queen of Italy on the wall.

"How long," I asked, "have you been here
blacking shoes?"

He looked up at me with his piercing black
eyes and an ingratiating smile, a smile possible
only to an Italian.

"Twenty-seven years," said he.

If he had struck me he could scarcely have surprised me more. Twenty-seven years blacking shoes; think of it! And all right here on this street corner.

"You must," said I, "have blacked a million shoes in that time."

"Mebbe—perhaps," he said, smiling until his teeth gleamed, "tinka two-three million. All pipple in city."

It was inconceivable. It defied all my notions of the city where, of course, people are constantly changing about, doing new things —and being rather miserable in doing them.

"Do you like it?" I asked.

"Sure, I like. I mak' money."

He said it jauntily; and looked as happy as a man could.

"Another ideal exploded," said I to myself, for my idea of the bootblack, as I think of it now with amusement, was in terms of the poor, starved, hungry street boy of youthful storybooks; starved to-day, but a mayor or senator presently; a miserable figure, through whom one could easily acquire, at trivial cost, the inner glow of the charitable. But this stocky, sturdy Italian had not only been at it twenty-seven years without becoming President, but

actually seemed to like it.   So I sat there mar-
velling on my throne, as surprised as the Lord
God in Eden at what I found.

Just then a fine-looking young fellow, extremely well dressed, darked-eyed and trim,
stepped into the little shop; and my bootblack,
pausing a moment and putting down his
brushes, took from his inner pocket a worn
leather pocketbook, and from a substantial
supply of bills took out three and gave them to
the young man.   As he turned back to his
work on my shoes, he said:

"He my boy."

"Your boy?"

"Yes, he go college this year; spend plenty
da mon'."

"College!"

"Sure, he go college."

What next?   I began at once to ask a
hundred eager questions.   This poor, down-
trodden bootblack!   Just outside by the curb
he showed me his Car; no very grand affair,
indeed, but nevertheless a Car, wherein he
drove to work in the morning as fine as you
please.   Turning over a new customer to one
of his helpers, he told me, as he brushed me off,
of his wife and family, and then, seeing how

deeply interested I was, he took from his inner pocket a couple of photographs (rather soiled), one of himself, his wife, and children, he with a starched collar and his moustache curled to perfection, and his family as robust and cheerful as one could wish to see.

"And that," said he, showing me the other photograph, "is my house."

His house!

He stood there smiling at my wonder.

"And you earned all this blacking shoes?"

"Sure, I earn. I mak' plenty da mon'."

Well, there he stood, a reality; to me, a new person; sturdy, vigorous, happy, with his cubby of a shop, his brushes, his car, his house, his blacked-eyed family, his son in college.

"I wonder," I thought, laughed at myself, "whether I am the Caliph incognito, or he."

"Well," I said aloud, "I think you have done wonders."

He smiled broadly.

"And I'd like to shake hands with you."

This was evidently something entirely new, but brushing his hand off on his apron he extended it to me.

"You're a real man," said I; "you're a true citizen. I want to call on you again."

"Sure."

"Sure" has come to be one of the most expressive words in the American language, said as he said it, with gusto and unction.

I left him there smiling broadly, with his greasy fat pocketbook just showing above his vest, and the tool of his triumph, his blacking brush, in his hand. I think he also enjoyed the adventure.

"Well, well!" said I, "if I haven't had my money's worth; if that isn't a story—just blundered into."

And walking across the street toward the wharves and turning these astonishing things over in my mind, and occasionally catching a blinding glimpse of the halo from my new-shined shoes, I said to myself:

"I like being a Caliph—as far as I have gone."

I stood for a long time on the docks watching a great rusty, weatherbeaten British ship discharging a pungent cargo of tea from Ceylon and teakwood timbers and baled cotton goods from India—and all in the clear May sunshine. A raw Scotchman at the donkey-engine bellowed and swore, and nimble little lascar sailors in woolly turbans and dirty cotton shirts darted about the littered deck. I watched with delight the husky longshoremen, their bare arms all knotty with muscles as they lifted and loaded and ran with the heavy trucks. I love the very look of outdoor men powerfully and easily at work. How deftly they lifted the great bales and timbers; and in the intervals how still they stood to rest. I liked the well-controlled power of the hoisting engine and the little plumes of steam, worried by a fresh breeze from off the bay, as they were torn in ragged gusts from the exhaust.

"What a world this is," I thought, "full of all kinds of strange and interesting people."

I had a great impulse to go aboard the ship myself and try to find out more about the Scotch engine-driver, the lascars, and the longshoremen.

"Each of us," I said to myself, "gets to thinking of himself as the centre of the universe. That great bellowing Scotchman clearly thinks so, and that little dark lascar out of India is no doubt sure that he is— probably thinks that all of us are in outer darkness; and that Jew, checking out the boxes of tea, is he not also to himself the centre of the

universe? And how am I better than any one
of them? Don't I think I am also the centre
of the universe? Now, it is evident that we
can't all be centres. There aren't enough uni-
verses to go around. If we keep on trying it,
I can see nothing ahead of us but celestial
collisions—and chaos. The question seems
to be: How shall we all learn to live together
agreeably at the centre of the only universe we
are ever likely to know anything about? And
how can we do that unless we understand one
another?"

Musing upon these things I moved on again,
thinking that one day I'd sail to India on just
such a rusty ship and come really to know all
these strange people.

So I came again into the streets of the city,
considering where I should go next.

"Sooner or later," said I, "I shall have to
honour some one of my fellow democrats by
having him take me to luncheon. One must
eat."

This idea amused me greatly, and I thought
of all the different ways I could try to beguile
one of these hurrying strangers not only to invite me to luncheon, but to be glad afterward
that he had done it. No problem that isn't

difficult is interesting, said I to myself, and to a true Caliph, said I, all things are possible.

So I walked up the long street from the wharves; and with the necessity of finding a luncheon somewhere looming greater every moment.

Presently I stopped at the window of a second-hand bookshop, quite a dusty, shabby place, but when I looked in at all the wares there exhibited I had a kind of love for it. I am not one who is much drawn to any book simply because it is old; and why such pother over a first edition when the same good contents are in the second or fiftieth? And yet old books are not unlike old houses: they wear upon them the marks of life. Often and often at a shabby stall have I picked up a book marked here and there by some former traveller: here a passage scored with approval, there one underlined with emphasis, or a word corrected or queried. In reading such a book it is almost as though you had an unseen companion looking over your shoulder, and before you get through you come to know pretty well what kind of man he was. Not long ago I found an old book in an old shop which delighted me greatly, for it bears the footprints of a

furiously angry man.   "Bah!" he writes on the
margin, or "Piffle," or "The Idiot," or "Soph-
omoric."   I turned each page with delight, expecting some new explosion.

(There is another advantage in old book-
stores that I should put in parentheses: there
one can get two or three books for the price of
one.)

So I thought I would go into the shop and
take up a book or two—luncheon or no luncheon.   And it was here that I met my fate!

Harriet says that I am lucky; that I "fall
into things."   But I think it is only because I
look like a countryman, and so, when I begin
to ask questions, I make the stranger feel somehow superior, which is to him a comfortable,
tolerant feeling and does no harm to me.   And
besides, a man has a kind of fondness for those
for whom, in his superiority, he feels that he
must   make   allowances.   I   know   well   the
allowances that have to be made for me.

While I was in the bookshop I noticed there
another customer: a middle-aged man with thin
grey hair and a somewhat weary look.   He was
taking up a book here and there, but hardly
looking at it before he put it back again.   He
seemed not to know what he wanted.   And yet,

by the way of him, he was a man of evident
position—perhaps of some wealth. He might
be one of those men who make believe that they
have a passion for first editions. I watched him
out of the corner of my eye.

"He looks," said I, "as though he were bored
with life."

It struck me as an inspiration, so suddenly
that I could feel a warm flush spreading
through my body, that this was the very man
I was looking for—to take the Caliph to lunch.

But how to do it?

I studied him sharply, pretending I was deep
in a book, and watched for an opening. There
were the little familiar marks around his eyes
that showed humour; and this was an element
in my favour. For humour is the world's
Esperanto.

Still I held back; and still he kept picking
up and putting down various books. I tried to
think up a clever speech to make to him; but
have never in my life been able, beforehand, to
think of anything clever to say. Presently, he
all but threw down a book, as though in disgust,
and, turning suddenly, walked out of the shop.

Though a Caliph, I was panic-stricken. He
was about to escape me. I saw the prospects

of luncheon fading away. But I stepped so quickly after him that we were almost face to face in the little entry of the shop. Now or never!

"Do you know," said I, "of a good place to lunch?"

It was not at all what I intended to say.

It seemed to take him a moment to focus upon me. I could see in his sharp glance the shrewd appraisal of the business man.

"Why, no," said he; "at least not around here."

"I am a stranger here," said I, "from the country. I do not know the City."

He seemed to be thinking about a place to direct me to. I was at the crisis now; everything depended on what I said next.

"I had a very amusing idea in the shop there," I said, looking him in the eye and smiling.

He did not answer, but looked at me again, this time with an air of vague curiosity.

"I am interested in books too," I said, "and I could see you taking them up and putting them down as though you were—well, disgusted with them."

Still he did not reply, but stood looking at me

"He was about to escape me. I saw the prospects of luncheon fading away."

now half impatiently—though a kind of amused
glint came in his eye.

"Who are you, anyway?" he asked, not ill-
naturedly.

"I am a countryman," I said, "a kind of
farmer."

"I can see that," he said, half smiling; "but
you must be something more than a farmer,
or you wouldn't be visiting old bookshops."

"Now," said I eagerly, "you are discovering
me; the fact is, I *am* more than a countryman.
I am here incognito."

"How is that?" he asked, plainly not knowing whether to be amused or irritated or
alarmed.

With that I began telling him how I had
started out that morning and how I had felt,
a stranger in the streets, and how that had led
me to the odd fancies I have already described.
I made the whole story, including my experience
with the Italian bootblack, as amusing and yet
as matter of fact as I could. . . . But suppose
he had no imagination!

"So you're now a Caliph incognito," said he,
laughing.

"Yes," said I.

"Looking for adventure in Bagdad?"

"Yes," said I, "and I want to tell you where you come in."

He now looked thoroughly amused—with every wrinkle around his eyes in full employment. Blessed be, he *had* imagination!

"I decided," I said, "that you might well be the citizen of Bagdad who would take the Caliph to luncheon."

At this he laughed aloud.

"Well," said he, "whoever you are, you're a good one. And why not? I was going to my club to luncheon; but when a Caliph is in town——"

So we turned up the street together. I cannot tell how triumphant I felt. It was as though I had won a battle.

He was clearly still somewhat suspicious—your true City man is difficult to beguile—and opened up on the subject of books, I think as a kind of new test of me. As luck would have it, he fell outright upon an old passion of mine, George Borrow, and I soon found that my friend could easily floor me on the early editions and the bindings, but that I easily put him down when we came to discuss Isopel Berners and the Flaming Tinman.

By this time we were comfortably seated at

an extraordinarily small table in a curious little
restaurant kept by a Greek down a side street.
The table was so small that it brought us close
together at once. I think, by reaching hard,
we could have touched noses across it. . . .

I cannot remember now one single thing we
had to eat that day—and that is unusual for
me. For once started upon our talk, or rather
his talk, we never stopped. And such talk,
and such a new human story!

Every last man and woman of us, in this
world, goes about in daily drudgery, a dim,
dull, uninspired daily life, expecting sometime,
somewhere, a Miracle; every man and woman
goes about among suspicion, and jealousy, and
envy, expecting sometime, somewhere, to meet
a Great Friend. . . . This is true.

I cannot here report the full conversation;
it would make an entire book by itself; for the
warmer grew my interest, the more earnest my
questioning, the more eager seemed my friend
to unburden himself.

"I don't know why I should say such things
to you," he would say. "I never before said
such things to any one."

"You can be free," said I, "with a Caliph."

The worn, dull look disappeared from his

face; he seemed determined to talk away all the burden of unsaid things so long stored up within him. His name was John Cross Pitwell. (I have changed it only a little.) He was a business man in a way a little vague to my limited experience; at least, he had large and often difficult dealings, and much responsibility. He had made, I judged, a good deal of money. But these outward facts (though I did not learn them all on that first meeting), once we were started, became immaterial. Are they ever really important?

I have thought since much about the man's story; and if I could boil it all down into its essence I should say that it was expressed in a single sentence of his that I remember vividly:

"I've made money. I've been what you might call a success—at least my friends say so—but I'll tell you the truth. I've never done what I wanted to do or been what I wanted to be."

And that is why, ever since, I cannot help thinking of John Cross Pitwell as an unhappy failure, and his story, though simple enough in its elements, a kind of tragedy.

He referred to the chance of his being in the bookshop that day and meeting me.

"It was a mere chance," said he, "I suppose, of this spring weather. Every year at this time I have a stirring of the old restlessness. I wake up in the night with a feeling something like homesickness. I have a kind of self-disgust, as though I had deliberately wasted my life. Often something I see in a magazine, possibly a line of poetry, will start an ache in me I cannot describe."

"I know, I know," said I.

"And that is why I avoid reading anything serious; I want something exciting, absorbing, that will take me away from myself. But in spring days like these it sometimes gets the better of me. Once, a long time ago, I did have a number of keen interests. Books, old books and first editions, was one of them, and to-day, as I was coming down the street, I saw Cahan's bookshop and turned in. But it only bored me."

"I could see that," I said.

"Well," he continued, with a short and rather bitter laugh, "you see what I am now. I am a stodgy, uninteresting business man, uninteresting to myself and to everyone else, getting old and bald"—he turned down the top of his head to show me. "I do what every other man

of my kind does, say what he says, think what
he thinks. . . . It sometimes seems as though
I had never lived."

He paused.

"We grow ashamed of the best things we
have in us," said he; "and fail to be what we
might have been—with a little more courage.
I remember a poem written by T. B. Aldrich,
which I should never dream of mentioning
to my hard-headed partners. I knew T. B.
Aldrich himself slightly when I was a boy, wor-
shipped him afar off. My father knew him
well. The poem I speak of describes me exactly. It is called 'Voices and Visions,' you
may know it."

"No," said I, "I do not know it; but I should
like to."

"Well," said my friend, "Aldrich begins by
telling how

> "In youth beside the lonely sea
> Voices and visions came to me.
> Titania and her fertile broods
> Were my familiars in the woods.

"It is a picture of a youth full of visions—
I won't bore you with all of it—a youth who

goes to the city, where for a time the voices still
follow him from street to street.

"Strange lights my errant fancy led.

"But he does not respond, and the voices and
visions grow dim—and dimmer. The conclud-
ing lines of that little poem are to me about the
saddest I know:

"Now one by one the visions fly.
And one by one the voices die.
More distantly the accents ring,
More frequent the receding wing.
Full dark shall be the days in store
When voice and vision come no more."

He paused, and we were both silent for some
moments.

"It isn't," said he, "that I have been unsuccessful, or that I have been soured by misfor-
tune or ill-treated in any way that I know of.
It's because the world is just plain—damned—
deadly—dull."

I cannot tell how my heart went out to this
strange, rich, unhappy man. For what does it
matter, all the "success" in the world, when no
longer "voices and visions" come to a man?

I told him, in parting, of my lodgings and of Harriet; and urged him to come and see us.

"We'll have some more great talk," said I, "about this wicked and miserable but altogether beautiful and desirable old world of ours."

I left him with an amused gleam in his eye.

"I'll come," said he, "I'll surely come. If you can be a Caliph in Bagdad, perhaps I can be a One-Eyed Calendar."

"No, you're Aladdin; you have only to rub your lamp and do what you will."

"I've lost my lamp," said he.

I warned him that he might meet other strange company there: Sinbad the Sailor, Jensen the Bookbinder, or even the Great Roc himself; but he assured me that nothing should stop him.

So it was that I walked homeward thinking this day one of the greatest of my whole life. . . .

As I was going to bed a line from a poem I like, a fine poem, came into my mind:

What is this world but our secret natures opened and stamped into cities?

III

THE MEETING IN THE TOWER

I EXPECT I was ridiculous enough in those early days in the City, even after I began to meet a few of the people, like Mr. Pitwell and the Jensens; but the countryman in me, and the countryman's inborn suspicion of the City, even the dislike of it, sometimes got the better of me. I was always thinking how much happier most of these hurrying people would be if only they could live in the country.

You are entitled to smile when I tell you that I used sometimes to go about the sunny streets rolling under my tongue certain fine old de-

nunciations of cities—with plenty of "woes"
in them.

"Woe unto them that join house to house . . . till
there be no place, that they may be placed alone in the
midst of the earth."

It is truly one of the joys of the country I
know to be "placed alone in the midst of the
earth," where a man can look about him freely,
look up at the sky, look down at the earth, look
and think well of all the things he sees, and
so, love deep. "Slowness," said Rodin, "is
beauty"—but there is no slowness in the City.

Another of these denunciations came often
freshly (and humorously) to my mind when
I saw the great rich houses and stores of the
City with the swift traffic rolling by. It is
from Isaiah:

"Their land also is full of silver and gold, neither
is there any end of their treasures . . . neither is
there any end of their chariots."

("The old fellow knew this City," said I to
myself.)

"Their land also is full of idols; they worship the
work of their own hands, that which their own fingers
have made."

I love these strong old words, and while I said them humorously enough, there yet seemed to be a kind of sense and truth about them. People in the City are worshippers of the works of their own hands, and come easily to forget that God lives.

("God said, the heaven and the earth, think ye that We created them in jest, and that ye shall not return to Us?")

But the trouble, these charming May days, was that the City appeared not in the least shaken by my denunciations. The woes did not seem to touch the hurrying people! The streets, the tall buildings, the little open spaces with bits of greenery, had a kind of indescribable brisk beauty which I could not resist, and as for the people, although they were different indeed from the country folks I know best— the Scotch Preacher, Horace, and the Stone Mason—I began to be more and more interested in them. I played Caliph, as I have related, in meeting some of them, like Mr. Pitwell; but with others I came into contact in the most ordinary ways.

There was Mr. Tuney, whom I met soon after I arrived. He occupied a place in the publishing establishment I often visited. He had a flavour of his own, a somewhat bitter flavour, quite beyond my experience. The first time that ever I went to walk with him we stopped at the top of a little open square where we could watch the people streaming by like so many hurrying ants, to their evening trains. I remember the shrugging way he waved his arm and the tone of his voice when he said:

"Insects!"

That was actually what he thought of human beings.

Yet I found him extraordinarily interesting. He was new to me, and he rather shocked me (we like to be shocked— in the right tone of voice!) by calling me names.

"Grayson," said he, "you are a kind of Don Quixote."

Not to be outdone, I came instantly back at him:

"Tuney, you're a kind of Diogenes."

Well, he was.

So I invited him to the first of the gatherings in our Tower on the City Wall.

It seems to me I could make a whole book of that one evening, if I were to tell all about those who were there and how they looked and what they said. The *reality* of them—all sitting about in the cool of the evening with the windows of our Tower wide open and the distant, drowsy sounds of the City coming in! I think I see most clearly the old Dane, Jensen, there in our largest chair, with his great china pipe curving down upon his breast. It had a little cover over the top of it, this old-country pipe, like a pepper box, and occasionally he took it out of his mouth to remark, "Ach, vell," or, "Vell, vell, vell," in a deep, guttural tone, full of comfort. In his best clothes, with his shaggy grey hair brushed back, he looked more than ever like Beethoven.

One thing surprised me very much: Mr. Pitwell, when he came in, at once greeted Jensen. Jensen had bound a number of valuable books for him, and they fell at once to talking of the lore of old bindings.

Mr. Tuney and our dry little Knightly, who is always quoting something or other, came in together, though they had not met before. Knightly often surprised us with what he carried about, all covered over with diffidences, inside of him.

(If only human beings would meet one another on the basis of what they have inside them, instead of outside!)

And, of course, Harriet was there.

In a company like this, of men so different, and strangers to boot, there was at first some ice to break; but long ago I made the discovery that the best thing for melting ice is warmth. If a man knows you like him he begins at once to thaw out, and that is the first step. The next step is to produce some kind of a conflagration which so raises the temperature that all those present begin, figuratively, to cry out, "Fire, fire!" and forget in their excitement all about themselves. For iciness always means that people are frozen with thinking about themselves, shivering lest someone take them for less than they take themselves.

It was fortunate that Mr. Tuney was there to begin with, because he and I strike fire on sight. In no time at all we were tussling furiously over the respective merits of city and country. As I think of it since, it makes me smile, for it strongly resembled a question

which once, long ago, I heard debated in a
country school:

"Resolved, that the country is better than
the city."

It began when Mr. Pitwell asked me, as a
countryman, of some of the things that struck
me as interesting about the City—"interesting
or different."

"Why," said I, "everything is interesting
and different. There are a thousand little
curious things at every turn."

"What, for example?" asked Mr. Tuney.

"Well," said I, "here's a very little one: I've
noticed that nearly all the wooden clocks along
the streets— you know, those that advertise
jewellery stores—have the hands so pointed as
to represent seventeen minutes after eight
o'clock. Now, why is that? Why eight
seventeen, and not nine o'clock, or twelve, or
four?"

"Is that so?" exclaimed Mr. Pitwell; "I
never noticed it."

"Vell, vell!" remarked Jensen, taking his
pipe out of his mouth.

"Try it the next time you are out!" said I.

"It ought to be five o'clock," remarked Mr.
Tuney. "That's the golden hour of the day.

It's the only hour anybody ever really seems to want."

"Nobody in the City," said Mr. Knightly, "ever truly looks at anything."

"But what does it matter?" retorted Mr. Tuney. "And what difference does it make? And why should Mr. Grayson here clutter up his mind with such worthless observations? . . . Is *that* all you see in the City!"

"I see," said I, "that I must dig deeper to satisfy Mr. Tuney. Well, take the matter of age and death in the City. That has struck me hard. With us in the country there is a kind of beauty and honour about age; and death is a pageant which has not lost all of its meaning."

("Hear, hear!" cried Knightly.)

"In our town," I continued, warming up to my subject, "there is one ceremony that it would satisfy your hearts to see. We have an official town cane, ebony, with a gold head, with which we honour the oldest citizen. When he dies it passes on to the next oldest. I wish you could have seen our selectman coming down the West Road not long ago, in his black coat, with the gold-headed cane in his hand, to bestow it with ceremony upon Old

Man Norton. It had been known for days,
ever since John Webster's death, that the cane
would be coming down the West Road; and
Old Man Norton sat at the window, looking
up the road, waiting. I saw him there, with
his white beard, his skullcap, and his dim old
eyes peering behind his spectacles. He was
ninety-three years old. They said he cried
when the selectman came in stamping the snow
from his feet.

" 'Where's old Mr. Norton?'

" 'Here I am,' cried the high, cracked voice.
'I'm ninety-three, come April. I'm the oldest
man in town.'

"Well, you should see the pride of the old
man, walking about with that gold-headed
cane. It has given him a bit more of happiness in his dull old hours, which he might
never otherwise have had. But in the City,
who ever sees or thinks of the old? Where
are they, anyway? Who cares? You elbow
them aside."

("Ach, vell," said Jensen, shaking his
head.)

"And death," said I, "is not an event in the
City, only an incident; to be smuggled out of
sight and hurried through with. Both life

and death, in the City, grow cheap and shallow."

It is one of the troubles with me that even when I begin with a humorous idea, I turn serious too soon; and to my embarrassment find myself making an oration.

But fortunately Mr. Tuney was there. He rose at once to the challenge. Of course the country had to make the most of the old people, said he, it had so few of the young! And as for himself, if he were having pageants, he thought he would rather have them deal with live men than dead ones.

"And how does it happen," asked Mr. Tuney, triumphantly, "if the country has all the charms you say, that the City should be so crowded with country people?"

Well hit—and a good laugh.

"Here you are, now, Mr. Grayson," said he, "living in the top of this City lodging, when you might be at home planting corn! Here we all are—enjoying ourselves!"

Well hit!

By this time the temperature had not only melted all the ice, but we were sitting about in delightful summer weather, coats figuratively off and fans going. Knightly had already quoted twice from the poets, and Jensen's pipe was smoking like a factory chimney. Pitwell had utterly ceased to be bored. As for Harriet, she looked delightfully alarmed—and afterward said to me:

"David, I *don't* see how you and Mr. Tuney can disagree so completely and call each other such terrible names and still be friends."

"Harriet," said I, "if everyone agreed with me, this would be a dull world."

Good conversation is like a brush fire: once well started the flames go every way of the wind. We talked of poets and potato-growing, bookbinding and bees—everything in the world! I cannot put down all that was said, but I must at least report Mr. Tuney upon the subject of masterpieces in America (I think in secret Mr. Tuney writes poetry!), because he spoke with the authority of a kind of minor prophet, say, Hosea or Micah.

"Trouble with authors in America," said he, "is that they don't put enough of 'em in jail. In old times they had the right recipe for masterpieces. They locked up the poets and prophets and fed 'em on bread and water, or drove 'em out into the wilderness—and the product was 'Pilgrim's Progress' and the 'Epistle to the Philippians' and the 'Inferno' and 'Don Quixote.' But nowadays, if anywhere a man shows the least symptom of breaking through the thin crust of civilisation with anything free, bold, original, instead of locking him up they immediately invite him to tea. Instead of taking away his liberty, they force more liberty upon him. They give him an automobile these days."

("They haven't offered me any yet," remarked Knightly.)

("Your turn'll come," said Mr. Pitwell.)

"They invite him to talk," continued Mr. Tuney, "to lecture, to visit innumerable colleges, chambers of commerce, women's clubs, and they sit hanging upon his words, although they care less to hear what he says than they do to see him squirm. The trouble in America is not that speech is not free, but that it is too free——"

("Hear, hear, hear!" exclaimed Mr. Knightly.)

"Oh, they wear him out! Everything that is fresh and original in him bleeds away in talk to audiences which want to be shocked just enough to make their return to their own strongholds of opinion more delightful

That's the end of *him!* What we need in America is to put the really promising poets and prophets in jail—and keep 'em there!"— Mr. Tuney's face was flushed; and he now brought his fist down upon the corner of the table—"Keep 'em there on bread and water."

I wish you could have heard Mr. Pitwell laugh at these savage sallies, and the rest of us with him.

I had seen our diffident friend Knightly sitting over in the corner during these remarks, slowly filling up with something to say. I knew that he was a writer of sorts, one who hung on at the fringe of literature, too good to succeed and yet not quite good enough.

"How would you favour putting the authors in jail, Mr. Knightly?" I asked.

"It won't work," said he, smiling. "Now, I'm in jail, and produce no masterpieces."

We all looked at him with new interest.

"How's that?" asked Mr. Pitwell.

"Why," said Knightly, "I'm poor; and to be as poor as I am is to be in jail. No, jail won't do it. I see what Mr. Tuney really means: it's that your poets and prophets won't take time to be quiet and dig down into life, get some vital beliefs of their own about it. They

don't take time to look at ordinary things and
ordinary people until these ordinary things and
people become extraordinary and so worth
writing about; and, above all, they won't wait
until they must write or sing or prophesy because it hurts them not to—and that's what
makes true literature, and poetry and art,
and"—said he, with his voice dropping—"I
think religion too."

There was a distinct pause of surprise following these words of Knightly's; they were
so unexpected, coming from such a dry, diffident, unassuming little man. Yet there was
a quality of sincerity behind them that went
straight home.

"Right," said Mr. Pitwell, "you're right.
It's as Grayson says: we move too fast in the
City to feel the spaciousness and continuity of
life. We see only surfaces. I can see nothing for it but to move out to Grayson's farm
and be happy."

"I invite you here and now," said I, "every
one of you. There's room in the country to
live, *really* live, and to look at life—and to
think. There's even time to be tranquil, which
is the rarest achievement of modern life. I
shall go back there as soon as ever I can."

With that it came upon me with such a sud·
den wave of longing as I cannot describe, what
Hempfield would be like on such May evenings
as these: the meadows there, and the trees
coming out in full leaf, and the lilacs in bloom.
And the fine work to do there under the open
sky, and how a man could be happy there!
And as I looked about at the friendly faces all
around me in the room, I said suddenly—for
I had never thought of such a thing before:

"Will you let me read you something?"

"Go on," said they.

So I opened the drawer of my desk and took
out one of my notebooks.

"It may amuse you," said I, "and seem even
a little absurd—I don't care if it does!—but
I've found a way of living a kind of country
life right here in the City. I'll tell you how it
is: For many years in the country I've made
a practice of putting down every day in such
little books as these—not diaries, but notebooks
—some record of what I have seen, or heard,
or smelled, or thought or felt, as I went about
my work For when you write about life, it
is a curious thing, you get a double joy out of
it. You sharpen up every impression; you get
twice as much living out of the same experi-

ences. So I have been going back every spring, while imprisoned here in this Bastille——"

("This agreeable Bastille," put in Mr. Pitwell.)

"——in this agreeable Bastille, to what I have written during many a spring in the country. In April here I had April there, and a fine April, too; and now in May here I have May there, and already I'm looking forward to June. Two lives, you see, I live—one here in this Tower on the City Wall——"

("Your agreeable Bastille," said Mr. Pitwell.)

"——my agreeable Bastille, and one in the hills of Hempfield."

"Where does the Caliph come in?" asked Pitwell; "you are not forgetting the Caliph?"

"That," said I, "is another matter."

"Go on with the reading," cried Mr. Tuney.

"So I thought I'd read you the very passage with which I comforted my spirit this morning. It was written only last year and almost on this very day in May. It's really nothing much in itself, but it brings back to me a moment of the past so that I can live it again. I call it:

The Bees of Hempfield

"This spring, especially, have I loved the bees of Hempfield; and watched them long and too ignorantly. Some future life I shall devote entirely to studying the bees: all the varieties, until I know well their wise communities and all their regulated habits and trim manners. Since we have lived and planted upon this hillside, the birds have come to us in great variety, and many small, shy animals, including a one-eyed rabbit, a pair of Chinese pheasants, and a family of grey squirrels—but, more than all else, the bees. For in making beauty and abundance for ourselves with apples, peaches, plums, cherries, pears, and all the small fruits, to say nothing of many rich and sweet shrubs like the bush honeysuckle, we have given a friendly welcome to the bees. We have made a kind of bee paradise. I forget also the alfalfa and clover in our field below, now near blooming, and the tall hubam, which comes later. I estimate the bee population upon our small acres on a bright day like this at not less than six hundred thousand to eight hundred thousand. And yet people will say that the country is lonesome!"

("Vell, vell," said Jensen.)

"Of these, of course, a large proportion are in our own colonies of honeybees; but we are hospitable and welcome great numbers of other bees of all kinds. Just now the rich flowering honeysuckles are veritably alive with them. That old giant, the bumblebee, is a noisy worker but fast! He averages twice as many blossoms in the minute as the honeybee. But his manners are far from good; he is rough, crude, direct—like one of our oil barons. He wallows over the blossoms, tearing down the anthers, plunging headlong among the petals, driving by sheer force through all obstacles and taking what he will without asking leave. Getting the oil! I have been watching him on the columbines. Here he is a regular robber and takes honey without paying even the usual toll. Instead of thrusting his tongue down through the corolla, and thus helping to spread the pollen—which is the price that nature demands from the law-abiding bee —he lights on the outside of the blossom and bites *through* the tender growth like a burglar, and steals the honey pot entire. Oh, he's a modern business man!"

("Hear, hear," cried Mr. Tuney.)

"How different the honeybee, how much defter and better mannered! She uses her brains to save her legs. She apparently studies each blossom before wasting energy upon it: hovering an inappreciable instant above it —does she *see* or *smell*?—and making her visit only when she is sure she will have some reward in nectar. I picked many blossoms which I saw the honeybees rejecting and tore them apart. In no case did I find the little, glistening, moist bit of nectar which the bees seek. How do they know? Apparently the bumblebee bumbles into all the blossoms without discrimination, and takes the chances of finding or of not finding a store of honey."

So I closed the book.

"It may not mean much to you," said I; "but it made me live over again that May morning in Hempfield."

"And it gave me an introduction to your farm," said Knightly, "that I shall not forget."

Mr. Pitwell and Mr. Tuney were both about to speak, when the door opened and Harriet came in with a tray. Some time before this I had seen her slipping out; and then presently, stealing in upon our conversation, came that most delectable of odours—good coffee. And

here she was herself with her tray, the shin‑
ing coffee-pot upon it sending off a delightful
plume of steam; and a great pyramid of
doughnuts at one side.

Of all the masterpieces of art in this dull
world, fabricated out of common materials,
what is there to excel a fine, rich, brown dough‑
nut, with just a bit of powdered sugar to set
it off and indicate its true inner virtues!

(I would also specify, without offence to
other great artists in that field, that Harriet
made them.   Harriet has a way with her!)

Instantly, upon the opening of the door, Mr.
Pitwell sprang up and brought forward the lit‑
tle table, on which Harriet placed the tray.
Jensen sat forward, beaming, in his chair, his
fat china pipe held unregarded in his hand.

"If this," said Mr. Tuney, "is what ordi‑
narily happens in the country, I surrender."

"You'd better," said Harriet.

It may be that common ideas, or a common
class, or race, draw men together; but not one
of them equals in sheer magic the binding
power of a good doughnut.   After this expe‑
rience I am sure of it.   There we all were,
picked up at random out of the flotsam of life—
and like old friends. . . .

The pleasant excitement of the parting—the visitors all going down the stairs talking and laughing; and Harriet and I in the doorway to see them off, Harriet flushed and happy as I had not seen her since before we left Hempfield.

Only Knightly hung in the doorway, and seemed loath to go.

"It has been so friendly here," he said, wistfully, glancing at Harriet, and then, after an awkward pause, he said, half laughing, "I think I could really write—if I lived in the country."

("David," said Harriet afterward, "in some ways I like that Mr. Knightly the best of any of your friends.")

So I put on my hat and walked down with Knightly. We talked on the stairs, we stopped to talk on the steps, we walked slowly down the street talking, we talked on the deserted corner while the clock struck one, we turned the corner and came, still talking, to the square. . . .

(And that, I assert, is the true way to talk—all floodgates wide open and the water pouring recklessly over the dam.)

So I came back through the silent, mysterious streets of the sleeping City. And I thought of all the strange life throbbing around me within and beyond the walls of the darkened buildings—life so little seen or understood, because so few men take the time from their eager money-getting to stop and look at it, and thus come to know it and love it. I said to myself:

"I will look through these walls; the barred doors cannot keep me out, nor any customs or laws exclude me, but I shall go in and understand."

And I went up the stairs to our Tower with a strange, deep sense of having had, somehow, a great experience.

IV

THE ICEMAN

"A MAN," says Emerson, "is like a bit of Labrador spar, which has no lustre, as you turn it in your hand, until you come to a particular angle; then it shows deep and beautiful colours."

I like people, all kinds of people, but especially first-hand, salty people. I mean people who have nothing between them and life; who, when they reach out a hand, touch things that have actual existence; who, when they look up, see life and, when they listen, hear life.

One of the amusing adventures I had in the City—perhaps because it came about with such utter naturalness—was that with the Iceman. I never recall it since without a thrill of enjoyment.

I saw him first in May. He drove his cart into our street: a great yellow cart with an arched roof like the prairie schooners I knew as a boy. I was on my way down to the printing shop of my weekly misery when he came in upon me. I suppose I had seen ice wagons and icemen a hundred times before, but not with the eye of enjoyment that I had that morning. Possibly it was because there was no other iceman quite like mine! He was just getting out of his cart as I chanced along; and there was something so easily strong about him, a splendid power in his great shoulders and muscular neck, that I could not help giving him a second glance.

His head, thatched with crispy yellow hair, was bare to the May sunshine; he had a ruddy glow upon his face and a rollicking look of the eye. A big, thick-chested, well-knit man, with shirt open at the throat and hands like small hams.

"Whoa," said he, swinging himself down, and the team of grey horses, powerful shouldered and shaggy hoofed, came to a stop.

He stepped to the back of his yellow caravan, took his tongs down from a hook, seized a block of ice, swung it easily out of the wagon, caught the hook on the scales, looked at the dial, and then, turning quickly to a girl who had just stepped out of a nearby basement door, remarked:

"Mornin', Maggie."

He looked at her with a broad smile, as though there were some good joke between them.

"Fifty this morn', Maggie? You bet."

With this he deftly cast his leather apron over his shoulder to protect his shirt, swung the block of ice upon it, and disappeared down the area-way, bantering Maggie as he went.

Well, there was something jaunty and clean-cut about it all that I liked. A kind of reality, a kind of joy of life! While he was gone I looked over his cart and his horses. It was a delight to see how neat and well arranged everything was: the ax, with one side sharpened to a pick, set in a leather holder, a place for the tongs and the pails, and the feed bags for the horses, and the blankets, and the coiled ropes—and from a hook in the hood the dinner pail of the Iceman himself, with his pipe and

his tobacco pouch in a little box of its own near
at hand.   He even had the morning paper stuck
in at the side of the seat.   He could not have
been more at home at his own fireside.

But it was the horses which most delighted
me.   Splendid great Percherons, with coats
rubbed until they were like silk.   Every spot on
the harness that could shine, shone; every spot
that ought to look oily and black, looked oily
and black.   And there were red pompons on
the bridles and many red and white rings on the
head straps, and brass knobs, so bright they
hurt your eyes, at the top of the hames.

"That man loves his horses," said I to myself.

Above the collars, on the outer side, were
brass plates bearing the words "Sylvan Pond
Ice Company"—and these literally shone in the
sun.

"Any man," said I, "who truly loves animals
is well worth knowing."

I don't know why such common things should
so delight a man, but they do.   They seem to
mean something interesting, alive, real.

I found I had walked entirely around the ice
wagon, examining everything closely, and was
just back on the sidewalk when the Iceman
came out of the area-way.

"Good-bye, Maggie; see you to-morra."

("I suppose," I laughed inwardly, "he knows all the Maggies in the street.")

He hung his tongs deftly on their proper hook, stepped on the hub of the wheel, and slid easily into his seat. The reins were attached to a hook on the roof of the hood. He did not take them down, but merely shook them.

"Hey there, Lady," he called.

The ponderous horses stepped forward, the polished brass of the harness gleamed in the sunshine, the pompons tossed, the wheels of the great cart thundered on the stones—and the Iceman moved onward to new triumphs, new Maggies.

I looked after him with a kind of amused longing. I had not said a single word; and as for him, he had appeared not to see me at all. But I went on down the street somehow pleased and refreshed.

After that, every time my work took me out in the morning I looked up and down the street for my Iceman. I came to know the time of his coming and going, for he ran on schedule like a train. It may seem absurd, but sometimes I turned out of my way to pass him, or

walked slowly down the other side of the street
to see him in action.

"He is truly a popular man," said I; "if he
were to run for alderman, he'd have this street
to the last vote."

He joked the policeman at the corner as he
passed.   It is something to be able to call the
policeman "Bill."   He flirted with or bantered
all the cooks, maids, and even the housewives in
our street.   Once, going by, I heard him having a lively set-to with the grocer's wife on the
corner.   At a distance I thought that it was an
altercation about the weight of the ice; but as
I came nearer, it turned out to be a heated dis-
agreement as to whether it would rain or "turn
off fair."

"Gee, it's hot," says the Iceman.

"Hot!" says the grocer's wife, "and you
settin' in an ice wagon!"

"Sure it's hot; and me carryin' ice up three
flights o' stairs."

I even found that Harriet had made the acquaintance of the Iceman—or rather with the
head of him, for she never saw anything more
than his head looking in at the little trap window where he put the ice into our ice box.   He
always wore a broad smile; and it was not long

"He flirted with or bantered all the cooks, maids, and even the housewives in our street."

before the conversation spread from such cogent observations as "How much, miss?" or "Mighty fine weather, miss," to the disclosure of personal history. I defy any one, from a President to an iceman, to resist for long the impulse to tell Harriet how many children he has and whether girls or boys. The Iceman had four.

The oftener I saw him, the stronger grew my impression of him as a kind of Triumphant Character of the town. He had, it is true, no outriders going before him with trumpets; but his coming was not the less heralded. I could see in imagination the wave of preparation sweeping up street after street; the Maggies and the Sallies fixing the ice boxes, and then preparing to touch off the latch or open the area door. I could see flocks of youngsters—both boys and girls—ready to welcome him wherever he stopped and pick up bits of the ice he chipped off.

"A truly public benefactor," said I to myself; "a magician," said I, "changing about the seasons and importing winter into summer."

My amused speculations continued for two or three weeks and I had not yet exchanged so much as a word with the Iceman. But the more I saw of him, the more I wanted really to know him; to hear what he would say; to try him with questions and ideas and see what had come out of all this curious experience of life. I thought it would be interesting to know the ripe conclusions of an iceman about the universe, the solar spaces, the immortality of the soul, and the price of potatoes.

For it seems to me that no knowledge is better worth having, or more fascinating, than the knowledge of how people have come to be what they are; how they have managed to live in the world. And when I see a man like my Iceman who not only lives but does it boldly, joyfully, with a kind of triumphant air about it, it seems to me I can scarcely wait to be at him!

But how to do it? I thought of a hundred ways of saying exactly the right thing first— which is a difficult art. It is easy enough to imagine one's self playing the Caliph in Bagdad—and who has enjoyed it more than I, or kept quieter about my failures! But really to cross the line into the soul of another human being is not an easy thing.

It came to me in a flash one morning, as I passed the ice wagon, how I could do it. The Iceman himself had gone into one of the houses.

When he reappeared, whistling, I was stooping over to run my hand down the leg of one of his horses.   He looked at me in some surprise.

"I thought," said I, glancing up at him, "it was too bad that such a fine horse as this should have a spavin."

"Spavin!" he exclaimed.   "Spavin!"

It was as though I had struck him.   His precious horses!

"They ain't a cleaner-boned animal in Amer-ica," said he explosively.

I smiled up at him and then stood up, slapping my hands.

"So I see," said I.   "I like horses myself, and when I saw that lump on the leg——"

"That ain't spavin."

"No," I said, "I see it isn't."

Then I remarked, casually:

"I'm from the country, and I don't think that I ever saw as finely matched a team of Percherons as yours."

I could see I had hit him where he lived.

"They're not so bad," said he, but with pride in every tone of his voice.

We had some other exchanges.   I inquired how much they weighed and how old they were and then remarked:

"I've been wondering how much such a team in the City would be worth."

Of course, they did not belong to him; but nothing could rob him of all the glowing pleasures of possession, even the delightful business of bantering a stranger upon the assumption that he might want to buy. He probably knew well enough that I was only "talkin'," and knew that I knew that *he* was; but when two horse-lovers meet in this wilderness of a world they easily set up a little stage of their own and play upon it. You need not think that he was idling, even while this bit of conversation was going on. He was pulling out blocks of ice from the cavernous depths of the wagon with a long-handled hook, chipping them deftly apart into smaller pieces (he could guess twenty-five or fifty pounds to a turn!), getting ready for coming deliveries.

So our acquaintance started. We had no more talk that morning, but on several days afterward, when we met, I stopped to swap a word with him, exactly as I might in the country with a friend passing in the town road. I have one great advantage in such contacts: I am from the country, and who in the City doesn't expect a man from the country to be a

little odd? One must make allowances for a
man from the country! I learned that his
name was Curtis Haley—though everyone
called him Curt—and where he lived, and how
long he had been an iceman.

"You must have hauled ice enough in your
day to fill St. Mark's Church."

(This was a huge Episcopal church we could
see up the street.)

"St. Mark's!" said the bold Iceman, with
scorn, "you can roll all the saints' churches in
the calendar into one pile, and I've filled the
dang-blasted lot of 'em clean up to the eaves."

He had a kind of hard, common-sense working philosophy of life, fragments of which I
broke off, as it were, from time to time.

Here are two samples of remarks I heard
him make at different times:

"What's the use o' kickin'? You gotta work
anyhow."

"A man's gotta pay for what he gets, one
way or another, that's certain."

I have sometimes thought of City workers as
radicals; but so far as I can see most of them
are conservatives of the conservatives. My
Iceman was an example: he was a Republican
without in the least knowing why. "My old

dad was a Republican," says he, "and it's good enough for me." So he was a Methodist; "though I ain't workin' at it." So he respected savings banks and Masonic lodges.

I enjoyed these little contacts keenly; I felt like a portrait painter, touching in each day some little new characteristic of my Iceman, until he stood out, to me, a figure of robust reality.

"I'm none o' yer factory hands," says he, "punchin' out an eye hole or touchin' a button a thousand times a day. Me! I'm free."

And free, indeed, he seemed: a regular voyageur. Careering through the streets in his great caravan, brasses gleaming, harness rattling—to cool the fevered brow of the world.

Finally, one afternoon I chanced on the Iceman just as he was stepping into his seat.

"I'm empty," said he.

"Going back for a new load?"

"Yep," said he, and when I intimated I was going his way: "Get in, pardner."

So there I sat up beside him in his broad seat, rocking and bumping behind the mighty Percherons.

"Curt," said I, "I've made up my mind you're a benefactor of the human race."

"How's that?"

"You're a kind of miracle man.   You turn summer into winter."

"Say, pardner," said he, "I never thought o' that before."

"It's a man's job," said I.

"You bet," said he.

"You're doing right now, every day, just commonly, what the greatest princes of the past couldn't afford to have done.   Did you ever hear of the Emperor Alexander?"

"Sure," said the Iceman, "he was the old feller that cried because there wasn't any more worlds to conquer."

"Right," said I; "but with all his power and all his riches, he could not have had done what you do every day: have his ice box filled in July."

This seemed immensely to please the Iceman. He slapped his knee and roared with laughter.

"Say, I never yet thought o' that."

"Oh, you don't appreciate what a fine and great job you've got," said I.   "It's one of the most interesting jobs I know."

With that I began to be genuinely fascinated —as well as amused—and though I had not imagined, ten minutes before, doing any such

thing, I began to describe the process of ice-
cutting, ice-packing, ice-carting, throwing in
all the dramatic or humorous turns I could
think of, showing what a curious and wonderful thing it was, all the complicated process by
which the ice of up-country ponds was placed
months later, as regularly as clockwork, in
every ice box in the City.   I grew strangely interested myself in the story; and wound up
dramatically with a picture of the fevered pa-
tients in the hospital, who tossed less painfully
because of the ice that the Iceman brought, and
the babies that were saved, and life altogether
made more agreeable to millions of human
beings.

Since then I have looked back with some
amusement, and yet with a kind of deep pleasure and satisfaction, to what I said that day to
Curt Haley, who sat with eyes fairly glued
upon me.   I can see now that what I was doing
was to sing him the Saga of the Ice.

"Why," said I to myself, "I was the Homer
of this new kind of war.   I 'smote me bloomin'
lyre' and made a battle that seemed hard and
dirty and long somehow beautiful and heroic."

I wonder sometimes if those Greek soldiers
on the plains of Troy would ever have thought

of their work as anything but hungry and hard—the humdrum butchery of Trojans—if Homer had not been there to sing.

It may seem absurd, but I've thought since that I'd like better than anything else in this world to be the Homer of many such dull but truly heroic occupations. Icemen, steel workers out on the tops of new buildings, a hundred feet from the pavement, risking their lives at every step, trolley-car motormen, miners, woodsmen.

Civilisation is like a great kettle full of rich life, carried by the whole of humankind. If one least man falters or lets go, or falls from hunger or discouragement, the kettle tilts and some of its precious content is lost.

I think I never saw a man more fascinated than my Iceman. It was as though he had never before heard of his own job.

"Say," said he finally, "that was some story."

"It's true," I replied, "every word of it."

"Sure it is," he remarked; "but who'd ever think of it?"

He rumpled his hand through his crisp hair, looked out toward the great fine horses, which were rocking along in a steady walk. He nodded his head slowly:

"Some job—bein' an Iceman," said he.

"Say," he added. "what's your job? I ain't never even thought to ask."

"My job," I said—and it struck me curiously, all at once; "why, I teach flying."

He looked at me wonderingly and a little sceptically; but I was as solemn as you please.

"I know I don't look it," I said. "But people often surprise you. You can't always tell what people have inside them by what they show outside."

"Sure, I know *that*."

"I'd like to teach you to fly," said I.

"Say, pardner, you're kidding me."

"No," said I, "I am in dead earnest."

"Real flying?"

"Real," said I, "the realest there is. In fact," I said, "I've been teaching you already. In the past you've never realised—you said so yourself—what an interesting job you had. You'll be thinking to-night, your mind will be flying to all the different things I told you to-day. They'll amuse you and interest you."

"So, that's what you mean by flying. I get you. You mean your mind flies!" He paused, and then added, "Say, you're the queerest fella I ever met."

I rode with him as far as the storage house, where he was to reload, and then I turned and walked homeward alone.

I did not see him again for two or three days, and then chanced upon him unexpectedly. When he saw me a broad smile broke over his face.

"Flying to-day?" I asked.

"Sure," said he, "turnin' summer into winter. Sure—beatin' Alexander the Great."

After that we had a precious joke between us; which, if soon rather worn, never lost its friendly usefulness.

One hot day in July the Iceman appeared on the landing of our lodgings. When Harriet opened the door she found him there, looking like a warm gladiator, smiling broadly. He had a package in his hand. He had discovered where I lived.

"The flying-teacher isn't home, is he?"

Harriet said she didn't know exactly what he meant; she supposed I'd been joking again; but she replied:

"No, he isn't."

"Well," said the Iceman, "I want to leave him something."

He looked embarrassed.

"They got a big oversupply at the cold storage," said he, "and told us drivers to take 'em."

When we opened the package later it contained two very fine muskmelons. A bit of soiled paper was pinned to one of them, with the words:

"From Cuby.   Curt."

"Harriet," said I, "this is surely an amusing world we live in."

"Even the City, David?"

"Even the City."

V

WE ARE THANKFUL

"Is nothing done
Any more for fun
Under the sun?"

ONE afternoon in that City—it was now
come to be the autumn of the year—I
was walking along the street looking in at the
shop windows, deciding upon many things I did
not want.

"Thank Heaven, I don't want that—or that
—or that."

This was an amusing game I had come to
play with myself as a kind of defence against
Things, of which there are too many in this

world. The idea had come to me first soon after we arrived in the City and I stood looking in at a shop of antiques, where there were displayed many ancient painted hat boxes, old brass bed-warmers, curious chairs, bureaus, andirons, and the like. I had at first a feeling of depression, inexplicable to me, at the sight of all these things; they gave me a kind of mental dustiness. I looked at them more narrowly, trying to understand why it was; and then suddenly it came all clear to me, and I said aloud:

"Why, I don't have to have them—not one of them!"

It may seem absurd enough, but this thought gave me such relief that I found myself laughing heartily as I walked down the street. What a nightmare—to own all those bed-warmers, candlesticks, blue and green bottles, ship models, hat boxes, spinning wheels! I had a strong temptation to go in and look at the man who did own them—and see what it had done to him.

After that, I caught myself often rejoicing, gloating, when I looked in at many a window in the City, that I didn't own *that,* or have to bother with *that.*

"I have too much now," I said, "to interrupt me. If I had fewer things I should be happier, for there would be more time to be quiet, and to think, and to try to understand."

("One grows tired of everything," said Virgil, long ago, "except understanding.")

This led me along to many amusing speculations (which I will not enlarge upon here) as to all the things I might give away, or at least hypothecate with some benevolent "uncle," and still be left with the solid essentials of life: say, ten books, a garden—trousers!

"An attic in winter," said I, "a hill-top in summer, and quietude in both!"

It was with some such grand speculations as these, which (I confide in you privately) I enjoy very much, that I was going along the street that autumn afternoon.

"If they would only put in their windows what a man really wants most!" I said.

At that it came upon me suddenly and with a power I cannot describe—how does a man's mind work anyway?—that the thing I wanted most was a sight of the folks at Hempfield. I stopped before a fine great store window, and there inside, as plain as visions ever are, I had a half-comic sight of my awkward country neighbour, Horace, with the familiar skeptical smile on his face. There he was, as natural as life, and as much out of place, among a display of rugs, curtains, and elegant chairs. I could even see his lips moving as he said, "W-all now, David," before he vanished in thin air.

I wonder, do *you* ever have suddenly a hunger for old friends, a vast unappeasable appetite for the very look of them? Do *you* ever feel that nothing will satisfy you but the look, the voice, the very way of an old friend?

It was at that exact moment that the great idea of having some of the Hempfield folk down to visit us was born; and it led up to the celebration of which I am about to tell.

From the beginning the City was harder upon Harriet than upon me, though she made little complaint about it. Harriet is country bred to the bone. I knew well her deep feeling, from little stray remarks she let fall from time to time during those months. Once in the spring, not so long after we arrived, she sat looking out of our high window over that wilderness of dingy roofs they call a city.

She had been quiet for some time; and then she said, wistfully:

"David, by now the cowslips will be bloom-ing in all the marshes.

"Yes, Harriet."

"And the shad bushes will be white on Horace's hillside."

"Yes, Harriet."

"We shall miss them, David."

"Yes, Harriet."

At another time, quite without any reference to Hempfield, she said:

"David, I heard a crow crying early this morning, just as at home."

I do not at all mean to say that Harriet enjoyed nothing in the City. She did.

She enjoyed many of the meetings we had in our Tower; and some of the excursions we took. She enjoyed the plants she started, with irrepressible zeal, in our windows: the tulips and narcissus, and later, old-fashioned geraniums and a fern or two. But, most of all, of a sunny morning, I think she enjoyed going out to market with her brown armadillo basket on her arm. She had explored all the stores and markets around about and soon knew many a market man by name. Mr. Bulger was one of her favourites. He was a great, red-faced, jolly giant of a man in a white apron. He sold fish, and he had three children (as Harriet soon found out). To watch Harriet and Mr. Bulger negotiating for a pair of panfish on a Friday morning was worth something, I can tell you.

"They will eat good," says Mr. Bulger.

"But *are* they good?" says Harriet.

"I warrant 'em," says Mr. Bulger.

"Are they higher to-day?" says Harriet.

"No, they are lower," says Mr. Bulger.

"How much do they weigh?" says Harriet.

"Just short of a pound," says Mr. Bulger.

And so, by gradual stages, until Harriet has the panfish, jacketed in oil paper and stored away with three carrots, a small cabbage, and a package of tapioca, in her basket. (Nothing ever scandalised Harriet so much as the price she had to pay for a carrot or a cabbage in the City—when they were free in the country.)

But it was in the fall that both Harriet and I found our minds oftenest turning to our valley and the quiet hills of Hempfield. It would come over me sometimes with such a wave of longing as I cannot describe that the late peaches would be hanging thick on the trees, and the McIntosh apples ripening, and the hives would be full of honey.

"Contentment," I would say to Harriet at such times, thinking to cure with words things that lie deeper than words, "contentment is as possible in the City as in the country. Contentment"—and I would slip into my oracular tone—"is a quality not of place or of time, but of the spirit."

"That may be," said Harriet; "but I'd like a fresh egg or two; and think of going out into your own orchard and picking your own pears and plums. And besides, I wonder how tall the hollyhocks have grown this year."

It was thus out of Harriet's longings and my speculations that our plans for a celebration at Thanksgiving gradually formed themselves. We'd have down the Scotch Preacher and Mrs. McAlway and Horace (and his daughter), if we could get them, and enjoy an old-fashioned Thanksgiving dinner. One thing led on to another, and it was Harriet herself who proposed having in some of our newer city friends to meet our old country friends.

I never knew until then how much I loved these old friends. As the time drew nearer,

it seemed to me I could scarcely wait; and
when at length we heard their feet upon our
stairs and the great rolling voice of the
Scotch Preacher crying out, "Well, they got
as near Heaven as they could," Harriet and
I rushed to the doorway to let them in.

We had literally to unload them before we
could get to them, before they seemed quite
natural, for they had brought an extraordinary number of boxes and baskets filled with
good things from the country.

To want one's friends near at hand—to want
the old known ones nearest—is there a finer
thing in this world? I grow positively hungry sometimes at the thought of some little
peculiar or particular way of a friend, motion
of head or hand, look of eye, smile, quick turn
of body, metal or manner of speech, and long
to see or hear it again; to see my friend repeat himself. And when I see him, how
eagerly I check him over to see if he is all there
—all, as I remember. Or, have little new
things crept in? Are these new things sad?
—are they strong? Have the old things
changed or weakened? Has some sorrow
blurred his beauty—some happiness vivified it?
Is my friend all there complete?

So it was in our room, there in the Tower, as we sat about—the Scotch Preacher erect in his chair, his stiff iron-grey hair standing high on his head, slapping his knee sometimes to emphasise a point, and Mrs. McAlway by Harriet, leaning over to tell about the Barnard twins, and Horace, tall and a little awkward in his "store clothes," standing by the fireplace (the fraud of a city fireplace!) smoking his pipe.

"I told John Weaver 's long ago as last spring he was puttin' in his oats too early," Horace was drawling; "but you know John. You can't tell John nothin'——"

Often as I sat there I quite lost the talk—talk anyway is a lesser form of communication—because of the intensity with which I looked at my friends. Yes, that was exactly the Scotch Preacher; yes, I had forgotten, but that was just the way Horace always carried his head, a little to one side, skeptically.

It seemed to me that they were better than ever!

I wish you could have taken a look at our sitting room on Thanksgiving evening. It was not only the things that Horace and

Doctor McAlway had brought with them; but I had written Dick Sheridan, whom we had left in charge of our small acres, to send down some corn and pumpkins and other appropriate things from the country. With these, and bittersweet and autumn boughs, we had transformed our room into a true country bower. Horace had brought a basket of the finest McIntosh apples that ever I saw in my life; and there are no fall apples in this world, it seems to me, comparable to the McIntosh—and these we had on the table, near by, where they could be casually picked up and eaten out of hand.

"In the country there is always enough of everything," said Harriet.

Harriet had worked out the whole dinner to a nicety, even though our cramped quarters offered many difficulties. No sooner had the last guest arrived—it was Knightly, of course (who will, I think, be late to his own funeral) —than the sliding doors between our rooms were rolled back, and Horace, Doctor McAlway, Mr. Tuney and I, who had been trained beforehand, stepped out and brought in the dining table all set. The audience cheered our skill, and Doctor McAlway, who had one end, cried out:

" 'There was a sound of revelry by night.' "

The only thing that Harriet would not trust us with was the turkey. She came after us, her face glowing, with that noble brown bird upon a vast platter. There were little sprigs of green about it; and it gave off ambrosial odours which renewed a man's youth, blessed his days, restored his soul!

Harriet had insisted upon having no hired help.

"What's a dinner for ten? If I could have Elviry Moon, that would be different—but these city girls!" I wish you could have seen the look of superiority upon Harriet's face.

Just as we found our places and before we sat down, Harriet said:

"Doctor McAlway, will you say grace?"

It rather astonishes many people these days, especially in cities, to hear God spoken to, openly, as though he were real. God has become a Hypothesis, not a reality. But when the Scotch Preacher talks to God, you know and feel that God is there, actually there, to be talked to. The Scotch Preacher does not hang his head, or whisper abject entreaties, or cringe, or apologise. He squares away his great shoulders, lifts up his fine old face, which begins to shine with a kind of glory, and speaks out to God as a tested, certain, deeply loved Friend.

The Scotch Preacher understands love, understands it better than almost any man I know: that love is not something soft, yielding, sentimental; but something strong, true, fine, upon which one can rest as upon a rock in a weary land; that its tenderness is not weakness, nor its joy selfish.

Something of all this he radiated there at our table that night: braced us, liberated us, made life seem somehow a worthier and higher thing than we had thought it.

I cannot begin to report what was said that night; but there was something about it that was infectious, that set us all laughing at everything and nothing. All the bonds and bars of strangeness fell down between us, and everyone shone at his best and keenest, because at his truest. I never heard any one tell better stories than Doctor McAlway—or laugh harder at them himself; or any one make wittier comments than Mr. Tuney; and in the mid-

dle of the meal little Knightly pushed back his
chair and stood up while he recited, "The
Coons of Cahoon Hollow."

In thinking of it since, I have wondered if
something of this freedom and enjoyment did
not spring from the fact that the celebration
was a true reversion to the youth of all of us,
the youth, the naïve youth—indeed, of America. No holiday in all our calendar is comparable to Thanksgiving. There is no holiday quite like it anywhere in the world. It
celebrates no battle, no fall of a Bastille, no
bank or business holiday, the birthday of no
great man, no political revolution, no church
ritual. It is the great holiday of common
people who have worked all the year and now
thank God humbly for good harvests. We
are not celebrating Washington or Columbus
or the Declaration of Independence—but just
the true, good things, the simple blessings of
the soil and the common life. Most holidays
are somehow pagan, and if traced back are
rooted in the dull and bloody stories of some
old war; but Thanksgiving is the holiday of
peace: the celebration of work and the simple
life. You must go back to the old Greeks for
anything to compare with it—a true folk festi-

val that speaks the poetry of the turn of the
seasons, the beauty of the harvest, the ripe
product of the year, and the deep, deep con-
nection of all these things with God.

Something of this came out in our talk.

"Yes," said Mr. Pitwell, "it is undoubtedly
the most American of all our holidays."

"Even the food," said Mrs. McAlway.

"That is true," put in Mrs. Tuney, "there is
scarcely a dish on this table that is not peculiar
to America, native to our soil—and most of
them can be had nowhere else in the world."

It was truly an old-fashioned Thanksgiving
dinner. We had many of the things down
from our own country, all the vegetables except the sweet potatoes—celery, onions, and
Hubbard squash (one cannot properly give
thanks without Hubbard squash)—from our
own land. We also had jelly that Harriet herself made, and honey from our own hives.
But the grand event of the meal was the
pumpkin pie. None of your little, thin, ema-
ciated, leather-bound pumpkin pies; but deep,
thick, golden-yellow, baked in a brown crock-
ery plate. Made of a special small variety of
russeted sweet pumpkin which Harriet and I
discovered years ago, a perfect pumpkin! (I

have told Harriet since that if she had not been born modest, the remarks about that pumpkin pie would have spoiled her!)

"I have not eaten such a dinner since I was a boy," said Mr. Pitwell.

"I have been trying to think of a really appropriate word for it," said Mr. Knightly.

"Delectable," said Mrs. Tuney.

"Salubrious," remarked her husband.

"W-all," said Horace, now breaking in—he had been pretty busy all along—"I'd call it durned good."

One feature of the talk after dinner stands out above everything else; and it came from quite an unexpected source. We never knew Horace had it in him!

Somehow, the conversation had turned on old New England traditions, of which Thanksgiving was so much a part. Mr. Tuney observed that it was rather a pity that we had not developed here in America, perhaps because we were so young, the folk stories and songs common in other countries.

"Why," put in Knightly, "there is no body of folk stories in the world comparable to the Negro stories of the South, and no songs better than the Negro spirituals."

"But I mean in New England."

Here the Scotch Preacher broke in:

"Horace, sing us the 'Ballad of Springfield Mountain.' That's New England."

Horace looked abashed.

"Go on, Horace," I urged.

"If I could sing it," said Horace, "as well as my grandfather Horton used to do it when I was a boy——"

"Go on anyway," we cried.

So Horace, with some embarrassment, cleared his throat, sat up in his chair, and began singing in a high, nasal voice (deliciously Yankee), with now and then a slide and a quaver in it, the mournful "Ballad of Springfield Mountain":

> "On Springfield mountain there did dwell,
> A likely youth, who was known full well,
> This youth, his age was twenti-one,
> Was Leftenant Myrick's only son."

Horace paused and looked around at us. He was just warming up to the occasion.

> "On Friday morning he did go
> Into the meadow for to mow,
> And as he turned around did feel
> A pizin sarpint bite his heel."

I wish you could have heard the unctuousness of Horace's delivery of the "pizin sarpint!"

"When he received his deadly wound,
He dropped his sythe a pon the ground,
Tho' all around his voys we heerd
None of his friends to him appeered."

Horace was lost in the depths of sorrow.

"This youth he soon give up the ghost,
And up to Abraham's bosom did post—
A cryin' all the ways he went,
'O crewel, oh crewel; oh crewel sarpint!'"

Horace, sober as a judge, had to wait for the explosion of laughter that here broke through.

"So soon his careful father went
To seek his son with discontent,
And there his onley son he faound
Ded as a stun a pon the ground.
His father viewed his track with great consarn
Where he had run acrost the corn.
Uneven tracks, where he did go,
Appeared to stagger to and frow."

Horace's voice now reeked with unutterable woe.

"The seventh of August, sixty-one,
This fatal axsident was done.
Let this a warning be to all,
To be prepared when God does call."

Horace certainly brought down the house.

"I told you Horace could give you a real taste of the soil," said Doctor McAlway.

But it was little Knightly who was most excited.

"Where did it come from?" he demanded. "Are there any more?"

Nothing would do but Horace must sing it again—which he did, and far better than at first, for he had lost all embarrassment and entered wholly into the spirit of the fun. If old Gran'ther Horton could have done it better I missed one of the great things of life in never having heard him.

Since then I rarely see Horace that he does not recall that evening in our Tower: it was truly a red-letter day in his life.

Once, before I began to understand who I was and what I had to do with this world, I was sometimes distressed by the problems of the Present, and concerned over the chances of the Future; but at such times I would say to myself:

"One thing is certain—the Past. No one can rob a man of his Past, or the happiness of it."

It was one of the early solid things I held to; for one can be certain of joys he has already had. How I have lived over again and again the pleasant, simple hours of our Thanksgiving there in our Tower: and the more I wear them with thought, the brighter they grow.

And one of the most delightful of these memories is the fine enthusiasm of little Knightly. He came up to see us a few days after the celebration.

"Grayson," said he, "I want to tell you I lived the other night. I really lived."

His eyes glowed.

"Those were great men you had down from the country: that old Preacher, and Horace the Farmer. They were not like our City men: all hazy, vague, all cast in the same mould. They were as distinct and clear-cut as a mountain or a church spire. Or like a great solid oak tree that has grown for a long time in one place, and the wind has blown upon it and torn it, and the rain has drenched it and the sun has shone upon it—a tree that has plenty of room for its roots in the soil, and plenty of space in the air to spread its branches."

"That," said I, "is what I think, too."

VI

THE MAN IN THE GLASS CAGE

"Man, if thou knowest what thou dost, blessed art thou, but if thou knowest not, thou art condemned."—Passage from the "Sayings of Jesus," his remark to a shoemaker.

I REMEMBER once a man asked me what my business was, and how the truth jumped straight out of me, as truth sometimes will, before I could think. If I had stopped to consider I should probably have said, vaguely, that I was a farmer, a gardener, a writer (and he would never have thought of me again); but what I did say was this:

"I am a man trying to understand."

I consider this business the most interesting in the whole world, though it never made any man rich, except in satisfaction. I have conducted this business for many years in the country, where it is possible to have some success at it. If one is humble and works hard and loves deep, he can come to understand a few simple things about the land, and cattle, and corn, and bees—and people. But in the City——

Let me tell now of a strange experience that came to me after I had spent several months in the City. I had begun to be superficially acquainted: I had played joyfully at being a caliph, incognito, in Bagdad—and I had made some fine new friends; but, instead of growing plainer to me, the City seemed only more puzzling.

As I went about looking, smelling, feeling, listening, thinking—as any man must do who would understand—I began more and more to sense a secret about it all that I could not fathom. Something existed here that we of the country did not know or feel.

Nature in the country responds to ancient reason—the slow logic of the soil, seed time and harvest, summer and winter, day and night.   One can discern a rhythm; and it is only as we discover a rhythm in life and move to the cadence of it that we grow tranquil.

But in the City nature seems all awry. Men have been cultivating the soil for fifty thousand years—who knows, a hundred thousand!—but great cities are absolutely new. The oldest has existed only a few minutes, as it were, of the ages that men have been here hunting, fishing, farming.

I found it rather an odd thing, as I thought about it, what a variety of reports of life in the City I had from the City men I met.

Jensen, or Mrs. Jensen, said it was "too qvick."

Pitwell was bored amid all this roaring life, "just plain—damned—deadly dull."

Tuney had turned cynic, and considered all these hurrying people to be "insects." He lived in a kind of metaphysical tub and went about with a lantern, not really to find an honest man but to prove that one could not be found.   Which is the way of some men with lanterns.

Little gentle Knightly had dismissed the complicated show and retired into the blessed haven of old books; from which he poked out occasionally to walk down the street "and laugh heartily at such variety of ridiculous objects which there he saw." He was the happiest—and poorest—of the men we had come to know.

Now, what was a countryman like me to make out of all these diverse reports? Why did so many of the men one met seem so unquiet, unsatisfied, apparently not knowing what they were doing or where they were going?

The more I went about the City, exploring strange parts of it, the more I began to have a new, almost uncanny, feeling about it all. It would come over me suddenly, in a street, up a stair, on a car, that the City was itself a kind of organism or machine, operating quite independently of these puny human beings that were running about its passageways or crawling into its little cells and burrows. No one of them, nor all of them, could stop it, or hasten it, or turn it aside—and yet no one of them knew where it was going or what it was all about. (I am trying here to put down honestly what I thought and felt: this writing will have no value unless I do this.)

Here it was, then, this stupendous City,

roaring and growling by day like some inhuman monster, and blazing away at night from
a million eyes. Traffic ran like blood in its
myriad arteries, and one could see the breath
of it curling out of its nostrils and drifting
away in the sky. A strange beast, this! Gone
wild, this beast. Entirely out of control.

"Why," said I, "it almost convinces a man
at times that there is something here more important than human beings."

In the night especially would this strange
impression come upon me, and I would find
myself lying wide awake, listening intently. It
seemed to me that the dull roar of the City rose
and fell like the mighty breathing of uneasy
sleep, and sometimes, toward morning, it would
almost die away, as though the monster was
settling down at length, with a sigh, to rest.

Then I would find my mind going out to the
country around about, just such pleasant country as I knew and loved, and I would see vividly all the loaded trains rushing toward the
City—with locomotives belching sparks into
the night—hurrying with the food of thousands upon thousands of acres of green countryside to feed this monster of a City. I
thought of the unnumbered men and women

back in the valleys and on the hills ploughing, planting, harvesting, to load these trains. . . .

And on all the sea stretching away to the East and South I saw ships coming, heavily laden, driving resistlessly through wind and wave, to bring strange goods for this monster's daily use or pleasure. I could see all these things pouring in to keep the monster alive— but what for? What was being done? Where was the monster bound? Who ordered all this?

It may seem strange that these questions should have plagued me (as they have perhaps also plagued you, at times), but I was a countryman come to a strange place and overwhelmed with strange impressions.

It was in June that my walks, mostly in the evenings or on Sunday, took me more and more into the dingy outskirts of the City. I had at first a deep interest in the people I found there, and talked often with them at street corners or in little shops; but presently the grim-walled factories there, especially a certain Mill with tall chimneys, began to have a curious fascination for me. Often as I went by I could hear from behind the walls of this Mill a kind of thudding heartbeat, as though I

were listening at the breast of a living creature. One place in particular, on a little bridge
over a sluggish stream, absolutely absorbed
me. Here, above the fortress-like walls of the
Mill, I could see a squat grey tower, or chimney, with a lazy reddish smoke curling out of
it. It was curious smoke, heavy, almost oily,
and at times, when the sun shone dimly
through the smoky air, having a kind of opales-
cence. I had been watching this smoke curiously the first evening I was there, when suddenly before my eyes the whole top of the
tower or chimney seemed to blow off and out
gushed—vomited—an enormous eruption of
flame, strange coloured and full of whirling
white-hot cinders. It came roaring with an
indescribable passion of force and seemed to
plunge at the sky as if to pierce it. It thrilled
me to the core.

And then, as suddenly, it disappeared; the
roar died away leaving all the sky by contrast
cloaked in gloom. It was followed a moment
later by the evil-looking smoke I had seen before lifting lazily, almost feebly, skyward—
the smudgy aftermath of a passion burned
out.

I suppose this spectacle was familiar to

commonness to the people of that neighbourhood, but I cannot describe what a thrill it
gave to me. It was titanic, diabolic—and the
more so when I remained into the night and
all the surrounding City was lost in shadow.
I could now see through windows or holes in
the Mill walls the glow from within, or the
light cast upward against half-seen smoke
from lesser chimneys. The walls appeared to
be covering, like a ragged garment, the
molten life within. It was then that the mystery deepened and the Mill with its thudding
heartbeat and its fiery respiration grew more
and more a kind of living thing—a terrible living thing. It increased and emphasised the
impression I have already described, of the
City itself as an organism or mechanism, created indeed by men but somehow alive on its
own account, moving and acting independently
of human beings.

It came to me presently that if I could somehow get at this Mill, find out what was inside
of it, how it worked, who said what it was to
do, and why it was doing what it did, I could
perhaps understand a little better the mystery
that was puzzling me.

I am a countryman to the bone; and in my

"The mill grew more and more a kind of living thing."

own valley, or field, or orchard fear no man.
It seems to me that every tree around about is
an ally of mine; the tall corn in the fields is
ranked like an army at my command; the wind
backs me up, the waters flow for me, the sun
strengthens me; I am like Anteus of old, drawing new power whenever my feet touch the soil.
Everything I see opens to me; every question
I ask is soberly answered. I have a proud feeling at times that if all cities were swept away,
all governments demolished, all inventions destroyed, I could yet cling here to my friend the
Earth, still draw nourishment from her breast.
We have been here a long time on the soil—my
race—and we would be hard to dislodge!

But in the City I had no such surety of feeling. I seemed not to have my roots down anywhere in firm soil. I seemed somehow overwhelmed; and yet there I was—sucked into the
vortex by the war—trying to understand.

I am hoping with these observations to ex-
plain the timidity I felt before these marvels—
a timidity which must, I know, seem absurd to
many a seasoned city man, to whom marvels
are as daily diet.

I picked my way slowly around the walls of
the Mill in the darkness and came presently to

an archway, through which, no one stopping
me, I went into the Mill.

I found myself in an enormous room, like a
great cathedral but full of rumbling noises.
All the machinery was powerfully at work, beginning at one end with huge glowing ingots
of metal, which were handled and rolled about
as callously, as deftly, as though they were
matchwood—crushed down, smoothed out, cut
off with easy but terrible efficiency. It was
such an exhibit of sheer power as I had never
before seen; and yet it was not what impressed
me most. What impressed me most was the
fact that nowhere at first did I see a single man.
Not one. It was uncanny. The machinery
was going as if by itself—of its own volition,
toiling like a gigantic slave with no master.

What a thing was that to a man whose mind
was stretched to the uttermost of wonder, trying to understand!

Presently I looked up. There on the wall,
high up on one side of the building, in a glass
cage, sat the man I had been looking for among
his levers and buttons.

"He is the god of the place," I said.

I could see him move easily, look out through
his cage windows, pull a lever, touch a button,

take up a telephone. He was as nonchalant as
a god about it, smoking his pipe.

I stood for a long time looking at him, fascinated, and then felt as though I would rather
go up there and ask him a question or so than
anything else in the world. I was so intent
upon this absurd project that I had actually
started to pick my way across the roaring building when I heard someone shout at me; and
then a hand, not too gentle, on my shoulder.

"What are you doing here?"

I looked around into a grimy face. I suppose a casual visitor in the night *was* unusual!

I groped desperately for the right thing to
say, and could find nothing, at the moment, but
the truth.

"I am trying," I said, "to understand what
you are doing here: what it all means, and
whether you know what you are about."

So often the plain truth appears ridiculous—
at first! Moreover, could there be anything
more affronting than to ask a man whether he
knows what he is about? While most men
don't know (this is a secret) they resent being
asked.

We stood there looking at each other.

"What in hell are you talkin' about?" said

this grimy man, roaring at the top of his voice to drown out the machinery.

The absurdity of the situation now came to me suddenly and humorously: my own ridiculous position not less than the anger of my grimy friend.   But I came straight back again:

"What are you doing here?   What are you working for?" I roared.

This seemed to make him still angrier.

"Me?" (I will here omit certain decorative eloquencies not found in Webster's dictionary.) "Me!   I'm workin' for me little five dollars a day."

I was about to roar in response that five dollars seemed no really good reason for working in such a place—it seemed a chance for an amusing argument!—when he informed me that they didn't want no blank, blank strike spies in this here Mill (I found afterward that they had just had a strike) and what, blank, blank, was I doin' anyhow——

I suppose if I had had wit enough I could have somehow got around this grimy man, found his human spot and won him over; but I didn't have, and took a roaring departure, with my host seeing me to the archway.   Here no playful caliphry would get me by!

I could not, however, dismiss from my mind the Man in the Glass Cage, nor the desire I had —it was more than desire, it was passion—to talk with him and see if he could not answer some of my questions. I felt that such a man sitting supreme above the bellowing machinery and controlling its least motion with a turn of the wrist must have precious secrets to tell. He must have thought it all clear! He, if any one, would know what it was all about.

A day or two later I went in to see my friend Mr. Pitwell, who, I felt, liked me.

"Well," said he, "here is the Caliph."

"Who, powerful as he is," I replied, "cannot reach one of his subjects."

I know of almost no man who has so much of the precious gift of old urbanity as John Cross Pitwell. In no time at all I was telling him of my experience at the Mill and of the absurd encounter with the grimy man.

"And you asked him questions like that?" he laughed.

"Yes; because they were exactly what I wanted to know."

There is a magic circle in the City. Within it everyone belongs; without it, no one belongs. Mr. Pitwell was within it. He not only knew the Mill, but was actually a director in the company that owned it. He gave me a slip of paper—he called it, smiling, a talisman—which, he said, would get me to the Man in the Cage.

"They've been having an ugly strike out there," said he, "and it is not surprising that you had a hostile reception."

As I was leaving, he said, half earnestly:

"If you get an answer to your questions, let me hear what it is. I have a notion myself that we don't quite know what we are about down there at the Mill."

My talisman took me truly into that magic place; and the very next evening, in a little dressing room just outside the Mill, I met Himself—the Man of the Glass Cage.

His name was John Doney. I had imagined him a powerful, vital man, with an eye blazing with conscious understanding of the great work he was doing. For how could any man sit up there year after year, watching those gigantic and marvellous processes, and not think it clear, not know what he was about?

"You want to see how she works?" said he, looking up at me.

"Yes," said I gently, "very much. I am

from the country and it is wonderful to me."

Methodically he changed his coat and lighted his pipe. He was a slight, rather pale man with a curiously immobile face and a tired look. My imagination, pouncing instantly upon these outer signs, interpreted it as serenity—the serenity, perhaps, of complete understanding, when all marvels are plain, each in its ordered place.

I followed him up the iron ladder to his cage, where he relieved his "side pardner," as he called him, and sat on a stool near him. From that vantage the great dimly lighted room with its enormous clashing machinery appeared still more awe-inspiring.

John Doney showed me, with faint evidences of pride, shouting at the top of his voice to make me hear, what this lever did; the purpose of that electric button; and how, with a motion, he could stop or start a fifty-ton crane, or turn over a red-hot ingot weighing a ton or more. But it was not what he told me, amazing as it was, that impressed me most, but what I saw as I watched him.

I watched him closely; and presently began to have the uncanny impression that he was doing these things without volition, moving instinctively, like a man in a trance. His arm went out here to a lever, there to a button, now picked up the telephone, now relighted his pipe.

"Why," said I suddenly, "he is as automatic as the machinery down there on the floor."

I looked at his eyes and had, in a strange flash of understanding, the sense that he saw nothing at all with them. He was blind! Blind.

The immobility of his face, then, was not the serenity of understanding; it was sheer blankness. It came to me with a flash that it was not he that controlled the machinery, but the machinery that controlled him. He was as as much a part of it as any lever, roller, pin, or cog. Instead of having his consciousness, his understanding, sharpened by the marvels of his nights in this place, his personality seemed literally effaced.

I felt such a wave of pity as I cannot describe; the shame one has in seeing the spirit of a man done out of him.

At the change of the shift, I went out with John Doney and sat on a stool at the night-luncheon place. I found him talkative enough, about his family—he had a wife and two children—the rent he had to pay, and his insurance; but when I came up to the great questions I wanted most to ask, I got answers that seemed to me curious and vague. Finally, I plumped the problem straight at him:

"Why are you doing this work, anyway?"

He looked around at me, puzzling:

"Why, I get forty a week."

"Is that all you get?" I asked.

"Yes," said he, "and it ain't really enough."

"But what do you do up there?"

"Why, you've seen it: I'm the control operator."

"I know," I said; "but haven't you any idea of what you are doing—I mean the whole big job—when you sit up there night after night? Aren't you *interested* in it?"

He looked around at me suspiciously, half alarmed.

"What do you mean? A man's got to live, ain't he? He's got to make his wages, ain't he?"

It was hopeless. And at that a wave of compassion for this man—this blind automaton!—came over me; and I thought that it would be the greatest thing in the world if I could wake him up a little, make him see what he was doing, the sheer importance and beauty

of it, the bigness of it. So I said to him
quietly, touching him on the arm:

"Do you know what I thought the other
night when I came into the dark Mill and
looked up there and saw you in the glass cage
for the first time?"

"No," said he, looking curiously around
at me.

"Well, I thought you were the most important man in the whole Mill. You controlled
everything. I wanted to meet you. I thought
you could tell me all about what was being
done in the Mill, what was made there and
why it was made."

The man's eyes were fixed upon me with
extraordinary intensity; his lips parted.

"I had a curious thought about you," I said.
"You know there are two parts of the brain:
the cerebellum is the part that controls action.
You are the cerebellum of this place. You
control it. If anything happened to you,
everything would go to pieces."

He was still looking at me with an intent-
ness I cannot describe—but now a look of
puzzled alarm came into his face. For just
a moment I thought I had him, that he would

come awake; but he shook himself and said roughly:

"Say—what are you drivin' at? You talk like one o' these labour agitators."

I tried further, but soon saw that I had lost out: he seemed afraid even to carry on the discussion.

"I got to go back," said he gruffly. "I got wages to earn."

I walked homeward in the night with a deep sense of depression; and in the following late afternoon went again to see my friend Pitwell.

"Look here," said he, "I've been in the office all day. Let's take a turn in the Park and talk."

This delighted me, for I had come to like Mr. Pitwell greatly; and so we set out together.

"Well, Grayson," said he, "how do you like our Mill?"

"It is one of the most wonderful places," said I, "that I ever visited. But strange."

"How, strange?"

"Can you stand a parable, a country parable?"

"A country parable best of all," said he.

"Well," said I, "you know I keep bees. I enjoy this greatly. They have come to seem like people to me. I like to stand watching them, or, better yet, lie down close to their hives, say in May when the drones are plenty and the young queens come out for their courting—and swarms are likely. It is a fine and wonderful society they have built up——"

"It must be," said Mr. Pitwell.

"But at times," said I, "there seems something positively terrifying about it: and this is what I am getting to."

"How do you mean, terrifying?"

"The bees are one of the most highly developed of living creatures," said I, "more highly developed in some ways than men; and their development is much older. I have read a good deal about bees. You know that they have been found in fossil form in the Baltic amber, showing that at least fifty million years ago—probably far longer—they existed in forms practically identical with these of to-day. Think of it!

"They have been repeating themselves, raising their queens, swarming, building comb, killing their drones, making honey, for fifty million years. Probably they have made and eaten a bulk of honey in that time half as big as the entire earth. Lying there by my hives in the sun, I have thought of this with a strange feeling of weariness: the endlessness of it, the ceaseless, terrifying repetition. . . . Fifty million years, and no change, no progress!"

"Extraordinary," exclaimed Mr. Pitwell; "it is something I never thought of before."

"Well," said I, "I had something of the same feeling last night when I sat looking into that strange hive you call a mill. I had a curious flash of wonder if men were not drifting into a blind alley of mechanism like my bees—where they would go on repeating themselves wearily for a million or fifty million years—and never come to know what it was all about or be able to change it. Among the bee people the organisation or mechanism absolutely controls the bees: not the bees the mechanism."

"Go on, go on," said Mr. Pitwell, when I paused.

"Well," said I, "I had an amusing conversation with that Man in the Glass Cage. I felt afterward as though I had tried to argue with one of my worker bees, coming in laden with pollen from a morning flight. I seemed to make as little impression upon him."

"What did you say to him?"

I told Mr. Pitwell, then, as exactly as I could, what happened in the Mill, giving the narrative a somewhat humorous turn.

"He could not see that he was the cerebellum of the establishment," laughed Mr. Pitwell—laughed, I could feel, partly at me!

To this I responded instantly, before I could reflect:

"Any more than you can see—you and your friends—that you are the cerebrum of the establishment. You do the thinking for it; and if you don't know what it is all about, or what you are trying to do, if you can't prevent outbursts that threaten the destruction of the entire mechanism—what can you expect of these lesser men?"

I was afraid at first I had hit him too hard. He stopped still for a moment there in the Park roadway, shot a swift glance at me, and then walked on again slowly, without looking around. I said nothing.

"It is odd, Mr. Grayson," he remarked presently, "how little we *have* thought about the larger meanings of what we are doing.

"What did you make out of the strike?" he asked, after another pause. "We've tried to treat our men well—we *have* treated them well —but they strike."

"It impressed me as curious last night," said I, "as I sat there in that magic room—it really *is* magic, Mr. Pitwell—the sheer wonder and glory of human genius: that it could build such a marvel and set it to work for the benefit of mankind. It is greater than anything Plato could have imagined or Napoleon brought to pass. You have built a kind of steel giant to do your work for you. It toils night and day, summer and winter; it never gets tired, It demands no vacation, it exacts no wages, it joins no union.

"And yet, as I sat there last night in that high cage, looking down upon that toiling but willing slave, I thought how it was that you, who have done all this, are quarrelling over the management of it. Not long ago you actually had soldiers picketed around the Mill to prevent some of the men who are interested —the workers—from breaking up or crippling this willing slave which helps feed and clothe you all. You balk it, you limit it, you misuse it, so that it does not begin to do the work for you that it might do.   You're wonderful when you invent and build; but how utterly you fail when it comes to controlling or using what you invent."

"It's true, Grayson, it's true.   But what is there to be done about it?   What will prevent these workers from breaking down the efficiency of what you call this slave of ours?"

"Well," said I, "I am only a countryman and know very little about such things.   But I had the impression powerfully last night when I was talking to the Man in the Glass Cage, that if somehow I could wake him up, and make him truly feel the wonder and importance and beauty of his job—if I could be the Homer of his war!—he'd be quite a different man: happier, and a better worker. What you need is a poet connected with your Mill."

"Perhaps," said Mr. Pitwell; "but he'd only make the workers more discontented."

"Well," I said, "I had a feeling last night that if I found myself becoming just a kind of cog or pin or lever of that machinery—an automaton—like the Glass Cage Man, I'd do *anything,* even smash the machine, to prove that I was really a man."

I had stopped in the road and found myself gesticulating like an orator.

I shall not forget the expression on Mr. Pitwell's face: smiling indulgence, puzzled concern. I could see that I was touching a sore spot, for Mr. Pitwell was a sensitive and thoughtful man.

"Well, Mr. Grayson," said he, "you need not think these problems have not bothered me."

We had stopped now by the side of one of the little ponds in the Park; evening was coming down, as sweet as only June can make it. I heard a catbird somewhere among the shrubbery at the pond side—strange music in such a place. Suddenly Mr. Pitwell looked at me curiously and turned the tables upon me with a question:

"Grayson, are you happy?"

This is a hard and sharp question to ask any man. But it is truly—as I thought afterward—the first question to put to the critic; for if the critic has not arrived at an understanding with himself (which is as near true "happiness" as any man ever gets) what right has he to criticise? I replied instantly (wondering since somewhat about it!):

"Yes, I am. Once I had a civil war going on in me, and I was unhappy. Now, I know who I am and what I am trying to do. I know what life is for."

It is only occasionally—once or twice in a dozen years—that two men (at least, men of mature years) get down thus into the very roots of things.

"Well, what is life for," asked Mr. Pitwell, "since you say you know?"

"It's to make better men, nobler men—and after that still nobler men. It's to throw all you are and everything you have into that one purpose. It's to understand the wonder and the truth of life—and then to make other people understand. It's to make of life a great adventure—an expedition, an enthusiasm. Not to blink sorrow, or evil, or ugliness; but never to fear them! If I could have made that Man in the Glass Cage see what I see and feel what I feel, his whole life would be changed."

Mr. Pitwell said nothing, but stood looking off across the little lake.

"If a city produces good and noble and beautiful human beings, then it is a good city; if a mill produces good and fine men, then it is a good mill. This is true. It isn't enough to produce steel in a mill."

I have felt abashed since when I thought how I orated there; and yet, should not a man, when asked, tell what he honestly thinks true about life—the true and ultimate thing it means to him?

We walked homeward, for the most part silent; but I had the strange warm feeling around the heart (how do we get these messages—by a cadence of the voice, a look of the eye, a chance word?), the warm feeling that this man at my side was more my friend than ever before. I liked him and had the feeling that he liked me. When we parted at the foot of my street, he took my arm—or just touched it—but it was enough.

"I think," said he, "you are right. It isn't enough to produce steel in a mill."

VII

A WINTER INTERLUDE

"It is good for thee to dwell deep, that thou mayest feel and understand the spirits of people."—From page 92 of the inimitable journal of John Woolman.

March 1st.

DID you ever love a little place?—a little town, where there is stillness and ease of the soul? I have. I know such a place. . . .

I have had a great experience, in which I have discovered again the beauty of the near, the charm of the common. At one moment it

seems to me I could relate the uneventful story
of the past three days in a single sentence; but
when I think of it again, warmly, deeply, and
my mind pauses with an indescribable kind of
love over each separate moment of it, I think
of a certainty I could write an entire book
about it. Nothing happened; everything happened!

I have had three great days at home in
Hempfield. I left the City last Friday, the
air murky, the streets full of slush, and came
at evening to Hempfield. And all about it
was of a whiteness and cleanness impossible to
describe; and still, still! When I walked
down the road the snow was heaped on every
side. It tufted all the fence posts, powdered
the tree-tops, lay deep and white upon the
fields. My breath made a plume as I walked
in the frosty air, and the snow creaked under
my feet. I had my cap drawn down over my
head and a muffler wrapped high around my
throat—in one hand my grey bag, and in the
other an awkward lumpy package containing a
bottle of milk, a pat of butter, a loaf of bread,
a wedge of bacon.

I cannot tell how eagerly I tramped down
the road that I might come quickly to the turn-

ing where I could catch the first glimpse of our own home. It was just in the edge of evening —you know, the time when the snow begins to look blue where the shadows fall upon it. But before I reached the corner I stopped there in the road, for it had come upon me with sudden sharpness that the house would be unlike itself—cold, still, vacant.

"It will seem an unfriendly place," I said.

But I ploughed onward again and presently the house came into view. Its eyes were indeed all closed with shutters, it lay asleep there on the hillside, no breath rose from its chimneys, and yet what a surge of feeling I had that I was come again to my own place! I made my way through a foot of unbroken snow to the doorway. A drift barred the steps; I tramped it down and came thus into the dark, cold, strangely familiar house. At first it struck a chill through me; but I shook myself, got a light in my own room, and went down on my knees at the fireplace. I built up a little live blaze among the old ashes. I ran to bring the largest stick I could find for a back-log and smaller ones to build up around it.

In a few minutes I had a noble great fire that lighted up the whole room and sent out a delicious glow of heat. I threw off my coat and got in more wood; and soon found myself whistling and presently singing, as I do when I am sure of my solitude. There is nothing like an open fire—the whole process of making it, poking it, mending it—to comfort the soul of man. There is nothing more friendly than an open fire.

Do you know the odour, the delectable odour, of bacon frying over an open fire? On a cold night, mind you, when your appetite has been whetted to a keen edge? The very look of it, sizzling there in Harriet's long-handled skillet—and oh, the sound of it—where is there anything finer?

I rigged a temporary hob by using the andirons and two pokers, and upon this I soon had a kettle of potatoes boiling over. Whenever the lid began to dance about, I swung the kettle aside until its fiery ardours had calmed down. I burned off the nose from Harriet's old coffee-pot; but the coffee!—the coffee was nectar for the gods.

Consider me now at my banquet table there by the fire, where I could reach the skillet handle—the room glowing with comfort—full of the good odours of bacon and coffee—the lord of all I surveyed. . . .

When it was over I threw more logs upon the fire and began to look about the place, renewing my acquaintance with many an old friend: a picture here, a book there. I think of all things in this world an old book gathers about it the richest mosses of remembrance; I know well many an author of whom I can say, as the woman of Samaria said of the Master, He "told me all things that ever I did."

So it was by chance there on my shelves that I came upon a set of old green-clad volumes, gold-lettered, that I have known as long as I can remember.

"Hello!" said I, "there you are again!"

I recalled warmly all the long history of those old books. They had belonged first to my father, and bore within their covers his characteristic book-plate with the blazoned motto:

The ungodly borroweth and payeth not again.

How well I remember seeing my father read those books—a kerosene lamp held in one

hand, the book in the other. Through the
long winter evenings! It was thus that he
kept burning the lamp of his spirit there on
the raw frontier.   In my early days, when any
book whatsoever that came into my hand was
meat and drink to me, I read parts of those
"Ancient Classics"—they had in them the
Iliad, Pindar, Aristophanes, Pliny, and many
others—and remember how dull I found most
of them, and yet how I persisted for the joy
of coming upon such marvellous stories as
Pliny's adventures during the eruption of
Vesuvius.

Looking at these faded old green volumes I
forgot where I was, or who I was; I forgot the
world, the flesh and the devil. By merest
chance I opened one of them, to find my eye
falling upon the rollicking chorus of women
in one of Aristophanes's plays: the one beginning:

> They're always abusing the women,
> As a terrible plague to men.

I read it through to the end, thinking how
utterly modern it was: these verses written
three or four hundred years before the birth of
Christ:

They say we're the root of all evil
And repeat it again and again;
Of war, and quarrels, and bloodshed,
All mischief, be what it may!
And pray, then, why do you marry us,
If we're all the plagues you say?

"Why," said I to myself, "that might be sung any day on any stage in twentieth-century America."

I had laid out serious work for that evening —for I had come to Hempfield on business— and forgot it all, forgot everything. I rolled up my couch up to the fire and put the old green books on the floor within arm's reach, and there, stretched out in a veritable riot of solid comfort, I read and read and read.

"Though care and strife
Elsewhere be rife,
    Upon my word I do not heed 'em;
In bed I lie
With books hard by
    And with increasing zeal I read 'em."

When I came to myself it was late enough, I can tell you; so I stepped out of the doorway to make my bow to the wintry night, as I love to do in the country. It was clear and very still. The frosty stars seemed low and near. Far across the valley, like pinholes in the dark,

I could see here and there the friendly light of a home. So I came in again to my own warm room, and it seemed strangely good to me to be there with all the ancient, familiar things about. I made me a bed upon the couch with blankets rummaged from Harriet's closet. After the lamp was out, I lay there looking into the fire for some time. . . .

"Life on any terms," said I, "is good.".

And so went to sleep.

The following day, Saturday, was truly a great one. I had plenty to do. Dick Sheridan, whom we had left in charge of the place, came down early, and we walked about discussing many things that must be done, such as the pruning of the apple trees and grapevines, the repairing of fences, getting up wood, and the like. I stopped for some time to look at my bees, safely hid in their winter quarters, each shelter heaped with snow. It had come off sunny and warm that morning, and some of the bees were venturing out to explore the arctic regions of orchard and garden. They are truly a neat and orderly people and lose no opportunity for house-cleaning. They were bringing out the dead bees, a single worker sometimes lifting and flying as much as twenty yards with a dead bee before dropping it. Often before going back in they would light down on the sunny snow for a minute or more. To drink? I do not know. Every colony seemed active and in good condition, which greatly delighted me.

I soon found it so pleasant there on my own land, even though the snow was deep, that I brought out a pruning saw and shears and set to work on my favourite McIntosh tree. I worked for some time entirely absorbed, thinking only of the task in hand, but presently, as I stood high up in the tree, I looked all about me, across the snowy countryside with all the farms about, and smoke rising from many a friendly chimney—and the cattle calling in the yards—and hens cackling—and in the town road the jingle of sleigh bells—and it came over me with a sudden glow how much I loved it all! It was something also, I thought vaingloriously, to stand up thus in a sturdy apple tree which I had planted with my own hands, so short a time ago (it seemed), and cultivated and pruned and sprayed. It gives such a sense of reward and possession as nothing else I know.

But I was not to enjoy it for long.   I heard
a wild commotion in the dooryard, and I
looked up to see old Jim Carter come puffing
and wallowing down the lane.   Behind him
came his son, driving his home-built contraption for "buzzin'" wood.   I had sent
Dick to get him, but had not expected him so
soon.

"Hello, Jim," said I.   He seemed like an old
friend.

"Hello there yourself," he responded heartily.   "Where ye been all this time?"

A big, slow man is Jim, loose in his clothes,
his face burned in the cutting winter air to the
colour of rich old leather.   He has the twang
of ancient New England hills in his voice, and
never fails to add a needless "r" to a word if
he can possibly find a place for it.

He drives the champion long-lived motor
truck known to man, so old that the engine
covers long since disappeared, leaving the
bowels of the creature shamelessly exposed.
When he starts the engine the noise is ter-
rific; one is alarmed lest Jim be at once blown
into the heavens.   But he isn't, he would
never go so far up.   His "buzzer," as he calls
it, is not "boughten."   Why should he buy a

machine when he can make one? What's a Yankee for, anyway!

He explained to me—I could not leave him for the very joy I had in watching the exciting process of events—he explained how he got an old automobile engine—"Cost me less'n twenty-five dollars—" mounted "her" on his truck and hitched her up to the saw. "She" is cooled by water from a vinegar barrel which stands just behind her and slops merrily when the car runs. Never mind, once the engine starts, the heat generated soon dries everything off—such is the cleverness of genius.

He has often to patch up his contraption, both car and saw, with bits of board, wire, nails, screws, bolts, a rusty box of which he carries always near at hand. To watch this huge man down in the snow and sawdust under his machine, blowing like a porpoise as he twists a bit of mending wire, is something to see, I can tell you.

I stood laughing inwardly as I watched him —or listened to him talking as he went along, like a surgeon cutting out an appendix. But, lord, how he can saw! "Buzz" is truly the appropriate name for it. His son passes along a cordwood stick. He sets it on the

carriage, drives it—zip—against the saw.
The carriage flies back, and he drives it forward again—zip—and the job is done. The
sawed sticks fly from under his elbow like dirt
from under Bowser's paws when he digs for
a woodchuck.

It is incredible that the contraption can hold
together to the end of the pile. It doesn't.
But genius, and Yankee genius at that, is hard
to beat, and a new bolt sets her going again.
Before I knew it the wood was sawed, and with
vast eruptions of smoke and steam the buzzer
set off up the snowy road seeking new piles of
wood to devour. Done! Achieved! Money
in pocket!

That afternoon I tramped over to see
Horace, and then around by way of Close
Valley and Barker's Mill to the town. At
every turn I came upon familiar views or met
men I knew. How good the flavour of the
place, how pleasant the remembered scenes!

There is a kind of sturdy humour in the
country that the city does not know. A
humour that grows straight out of the soil.
There may be wit in the city, but wit deals with
words: humour with life. I was amused at
Horace's observation regarding his visit to the

City, when he spent Thanksgiving with us.
He had enjoyed every minute of it, said he;
but, "I was glad to git home agin where people understand my jokes." (Humour, when
you come to think of it, is the very last thing
we come to understand in a foreign place or
a foreign language. Conrad, great writer as
he was, could do everything in English except
joke in it.)

As I tramped, it seemed to me that I never
had seen such a stir of vigorous outdoor life,
sharpened and vivified by the sun and the wind
of winter. Stories sprang up by magic on
every side.

It was the time when teamsters were drawing wood into the town from the Burnham
Hills and Crewsbury. Most of them had been
down in the forenoon loaded, and were now on
their way back. There was something so
jaunty and bold about these robust teamsters
with their fine great horses swinging along the
snowy roads that I could not help stopping to
watch them. I liked the very sight of them.

Presently, as I tramped, I heard someone
sing out my name.

"Hi there!" said he.

So I turned about to see a young farmer I

"Presently I heard someone sing out my name."

know, named Larkin, mounted upon his empty sled. He waved me a grand salute, which I returned. He came to a stop with jingling bells, near me, and I mounted beside him on his rack.

"Git up there!" he called to his horses, and in a moment we were whirling up the road—the sun glinting on the shining brasses of the harness and the red pompons dancing on the horses' heads. Occasionally a ball of snow cast by the horses' hoofs would come whirling back into the sled, and the sunny air was full of fine, sharp ice crystals that stung our faces or felt like pepper in our nostrils. And all about, sunshine and wide snowy fields, and a sky above as blue and clear as a man ever saw. Who can describe such a winter day! How it makes the blood race in one's veins and all the earth appear inexpressibly beautiful.

A log chain was dragging behind the sled, polished to a silvery perfection and jingling in a note lower than that of the bells of the harness. Larkin stood sturdily erect, his feet braced apart, the reins in his hands, swaying to the motion of the empty rack. His collie dog, which had come down in the morning, no doubt, walking sedately enough behind the loaded sled, was now mounted grandly upon the rack beside his master, head and tail up, nose to the wind, sharing the exhilaration of the moment. Once he barked in sheer lordly pride at a humble fellow-dog he saw afoot. It is something to be a dog on such a day!

Larkin, in his felt boots and sheepskin jacket, has made his sled a veritable travelling caravansary with all the trappings of a far journey. He comes a forenoon from Crewsbury and must want for nothing. At the top of one of the rack stakes is the battered pail for watering the horses. It gleams in the sun and gives off its own rattling music. On another stake hangs the humble necessary shovel to dig the runners out of the snow if by chance they should be caught. On two other stakes are the great woollen mittens of the driver, lifting, as it were, eager hands to the sky. Here are all the horse blankets, folded for a seat for Larkin when he has passed entirely out of the town, here the horses' nosebags, now empty of oats—like the driver's dinner pail.

We talked on the way, in shouts, exchanging news of the town. And so came to the hill above Barker's Mill.

"Got a good one on Sam Kennedy," said Larkin.

"What's that?" I asked.

"Ye see," said Larkin, "Sam's gone and got him one o' these here new motor trucks, and after the big snow the other night he couldn't get her up the hill. So he gets out early and ploughs all the snow off the road from his place down to the corners. But we're all drawin' wood these days, and so, soon's he got away, John Blair and George Broderick, and a lot of us, got out and ploughed all the snow back on again. You ought to see Sam when he comes up again with his fancy truck. Mad!"

"Well, what happened?" I asked.

"Say," said Larkin, "this is a free country, ain't it? Majority rules, don't it?"

At the upper turning I left Larkin, and within half a mile ran across Jabez Parkinson. He lives on one of the stoniest hills in all Crewsbury; and likes, I fully believe, to be joked about it. So I joked him as we walked along together. I remembered a story he once told me about old Jed Snow, and I wondered if I could not somehow touch the right trigger to set him off upon it. It took some manœuvring, but at last his eye began to twinkle.

"Stuns, ye say! Wall!"

Then he pursed up his lips, and I knew I
had him!

"Ever hear tell of old Jed Snow? Talk o'
stunny farms. Old Jed had the durndest
stunniest farm ye ever saw. But he was a
worker, Jed was. First year he built a good
big stun wall clear round the place. But when
he was a-ploughin' that fall, he turned up more
stuns than ever; so he took an' built cross
walls, so's to divide his farm into four parts.
Big walls they was, too. Third year seem's if
he found more stuns than ever he found before. So he just took and throwed 'em into
the four fields until he'd filled 'em all up level
—I jing!"

I thought, as I walked along, laughing to
myself, that it was worth a trip to Hempfield
to hear Old Man Parkinson wind up a yarn
with "I jing."

That night I had supper with Horace and a
fine evening of good talk, stumbling home late
through the snow to build up again my open
fire and fall into the dreamless sleep of sheer
physical weariness beside it.

On Sunday morning, I walked into town

and went to the church to hear the Scotch
Preacher. He grows older, but never loses
the fire of his spirit. I will not here attempt
to tell of all the old friends I met—who inquired, to the last one of them, for Harriet—
nor of the services there, nor of the Scotch
Preacher's sermon. All this would take a
chapter in itself. But as I walked homeward
again I suddenly said aloud:

"After all, life is the thing. The greatest
art of all is the art of living."

It seemed to me, and not without a mo-
mentary sense of depression, that writing and
painting and carving and acting—all the arts
—were poor business indeed compared with
this tremendous art, set forth so nobly by the
Scotch Preacher, of making something out of
the hard, tough, cross-grained material of human life as it was lived among these hills.

I had a fine great visit that afternoon with
the Scotch Preacher and his wife (I stayed to
supper) and came back late for another delightful evening by my own fire.

In the morning—this was Monday—I
packed the books I wanted and began putting
the house in shape to leave. And here is
where I missed Harriet terribly. As long as

the clean dishes hold out I get on reasonably
well, but it is not long before complications begin to arise. I run out of cups or forks. I
begin to feel big and clumsy; I tip things over,
spill the sugar and the flour, get things wet
and can find nothing to wipe them on. All
the towels degenerate mysteriously into wet
wads, the coffee-pot gets lost under the table,
the butter melts down, and the bacon burns!

"Harriet," said I, when I got back, "I'm
mighty glad to see you."

Surely I never spent a finer three days in all
my life.

VIII

COLOURED

And herein lies the tragedy of the age: not that men are poor,—all men know something of poverty; not that men are wicked,—who is good? not that men are ignorant,— what is truth? Nay, but that men know so little of men. —W. E. B. Dubois.

I HAVE in my life had much enjoyment out of Negroes; and several I know I have liked well and esteemed my friends. Something joyous, amusing, tuneful—some agreeable variety—would go out of American life if we had no Negroes in it. We are a sober folk, we white people; and look too solemnly at life. In many of my walks, these days, in the

City, or when I stand to look as people go by, I have reflected upon how rare indeed it is to see a happy face (much less a tranquil one), a face that seems to suggest an enjoying spirit.

So it was that yesterday, in the noon hour, I was amused and delighted at the sight of a group of Negro teamsters who had gathered by the side of the street to eat their lunch. They had left their horses with heads comfortably ensconced in oat bags, and blankets thrown over their rumps—for the day was cool and raw—and were now gathered in a somewhat sheltered spot where there was open ground—a few vacant lots, shelving off into a ravine.

They had either brought along or gathered up a number of wooden boxes, sticks, bits of old furniture, and had built up a brightly blazing fire. Two or three of them were sitting on the ground with their dinner-pails between their knees, but most of them were standing about the fire. Just as I chanced along, one of them suddenly executed a kind of buck-and-wing dance and burst out in a clear, tuneful voice:

"She's mah Lindy, Lindy Lu——"

Two or three of the other men seemed to stir irresistibly to the harmony, and when the bit of song stopped it was followed by an infectious laugh all around. I could see white teeth gleaming; and there was a quality of real joyfulness in the tones of the voices and the look of the eyes. I couldn't help liking it, or thinking that a similar number of white teamsters would probably each be sitting by his wagon eating his lunch morosely alone. But here, by magic, these Negroes had made a little camp in the jungle of the city, built up a friendly fire, and in a moment thrown off the work and worries of the day.

"They have," said I, "one genius not sufficiently prized in this world of ours—a genius we jeer at—the genius of knowing how to enjoy themselves."

This idea pleased me so much that I stopped a little way up the street to look at them again. One of them had begun telling a story of some sort; if I could not quite get the words the gusto of the tones reached me, and from time to time all the others would burst out laughing, slap their legs, or poke one another in the ribs.

When he had finished, another, younger man, broke in with an equally convulsing narrative, which he dramatised with head, eyes, hands, feet, in a way delightful to see.

"They have another secret," said I, "they know how to enjoy one another. I wonder if these are not the qualities which make the Negro, unlike the Indian, thrive and increase even in an unfriendly environment."

I began to wish I could drop in easily upon the group and talk with them, human being to human being, and was considering how it could be done without breaking the unconscious charm (I doubt whether it could be done by any white man), when the whistles blew, and the Negroes, kicking apart the embers of their fire (not too promptly), went back to their wagons. But even then they did not stop their banter. While they untied the nose-bags of the horses, drew off the blankets, and climbed into their seats, they were still shouting and laughing at one another, as though something about life was irrepressibly amusing. I walked onward again, smiling at what I had seen, and all that afternoon, at my work, had the odd, subconscious feeling that I had had an amusing experience and that the world was a gayer place than it sometimes seemed. A bit of colour and harmony in a drab street!

Where I live in the country we have quite a number of coloured people around about, and from time to time I have had certain of them helping me on my land. I am fond of talking with them; for there is scarcely a man among them who has not a gift of original humour or a touch of dramatic imagination. They are able to extract interest, amusement, and even a kind of beauty, out of the simplest incidents; to be happy with little. A Negro can do more with little, and less with much, than any man I know.

Two summers ago hay weather with us in July was extremely hot, and a teamster for one of my near neighbours—a good man, too —forced his fine team of horses a little too hard, and one of them dropped dead in the field. It was a severe loss to him. A couple of days later I met my neighbour in the town road and upon my inquiry and expression of sympathy he responded:

"Yes, Black Bill kicked off. I'll cost me all of three hundred dollars."

That was all there was to it; and I remember

thinking afterward that there was not a little of admirable New England sententiousness and stoicism in this remark—real Yankee. It was a stiff loss; but why make a fuss about it?

It so happened that the next spring I had a Negro ploughman smooth-harrowing a plot of ground where we were to plant onions. One morning, when I saw him coming down the lane, I thought something was wrong with him.

"Ah'm in trouble, Mr. Grayson," said he.

"How is that?" I asked.

"Ah lost mah bes' horse las' night."

"How did that happen?"

"'Long 'bout three o'clock in the mawnin' I heard a poundin' and a knockin' in the barn. I says to my wife, 'What's that?' She says, 'I don' know.' So I gits up and listens; and all the time I could hear that poundin' and knockin' in the night. So I says:

"'I reckon Jake has cast hisself and got caught in his halter.'

"I ain't never dreamed there was nothin' wrong. So I gits up and goes out with mah lantern; and all the time that knockin' an' poundin' out there in the dark.

"When I opens the do' an' holds up the light, there I see mah horse Jake a-lyin' on the flo', a-kickin' and a-poundin'. When I gits in he raises up his head and looks at me.

" 'Git up,' says I to him.

"He only looks at me—sad.

" 'What's the matter with you?' I says.

"I kicks him with mah foot, and I says, 'Git up thar!'

"But he only looks at me again—sad—and then begins a-shakin' an' a-tremblin' like a leaf. Then I hears him draw a long breath in his throat—like he was sighin'—and he tries to raise his head again to look at me. But he can't.

" 'What's the matter, Jake?' says I, cryin'.

"But he only throws out his legs and shakes and shivers all over—and dies—poof—like that."

The old man shook his head sorrowfully.

"Jake was a good horse, Mr. Grayson; he was the bes' horse in this town."

I cannot convey the feeling—the sheer drama—that my Negro harrower put into this simple story; or the way in which he used his eyes and hands, nodded his head, modulated his voice, while he was telling it. The tears came into his eyes. He must also have felt keenly the monetary loss, for he is a poor man, but he never thought to mention it. I could not help thinking of the extraordinary difference between the way the white man and the Negro took their loss.

When I was a boy and lived in a town in the North we had one Negro family there. Most small towns in the North I knew had at least one. We called this man, "Negro Joe," and he was the cause of much mirth and many stories. He was a whitewasher, or, if there was no whitewashing to do, he could clean a chimney—standing on the roof of the house and singing a song while he worked; or he could paint a barn, or dig a garden, or build, poorly enough, a stone wall.

He also performed a highly valuable public service in a thrifty town like ours, where poverty was unknown, of furnishing a safety valve for our pent-up benevolence. Whenever we wanted to give to the poor—as we were enjoined to do upon high authority—there was Negro Joe. We could pick on him! He had a large, comfortable wife, with a great rolling chin, rolling bosom, rolling hips (Joe was slim), and two or three children, who

easily adapted themselves to the part they had
to play in the town.   And their small house on
the edge of the village—I visited it more than
once—was a true museum of antiquity, with
many an ancient chair, picture, rug.

A trained eye could tell where each thing
came from: this had been Old Lady Morton's,
that was from the Barbours'; these pictures,
"Wide Awake" and "Fast Asleep," had hung
for years in the Cashmans' back parlour—until the old gentleman Cashman began to get
rich and his daughter Stella came back from
school with new notions of furnishing.

Negro Joe and his family were thus valuable adjuncts of the town; but, like many
treasures, we did not fully appreciate them
until suddenly, one day, Negro Joe announced
his intention of "movin'."

"Yes," said he, "Ah'm goin' to move."

No one could make out what the reason was;
but, like everything else that Joe did, it was
somehow amusing and dramatic.   We did not
at first think it anything but talk; but Joe
meant what he said, posted an auction bill on
the signboard of the town hall, and put up a
"For Sale" notice on the little house.

I don't know quite who originated the idea.

or how much of it was due to real regret, and
how much to a desire to have a little more fun
out of Negro Joe before he left; but one summer evening, almost spontaneously, a group of
young people, led by a harum-scarum young
lawyer named Cochran, started down to Negro
Joe's home.   They had secured somewhere an
enormous wooden cane with cheap silvered
bands around the handle; and this they had
tied up with ribbons.

I shall never forget the scene when that
little party filed into Negro Joe's front room;
all by agreement as solemn as judges.   I recall thinking at the time that not a man in town
could have carried off the business of wel-
coming his visitors with more dignified hos-
pitality than Negro Joe.

"Won't you res' your hat?" said Negro Joe.
"Mister Cor'cran, you sit here in de big chair;
an' you, Mister Morgan, do mah home the
honour of sittin' here by de organ."

Our young lawyer began his speech in the
finest mood of burlesque, expressing the profound regret of the town at the loss of its
prized citizen.   For ten years he had lived
among us; his life an open book.   We were
dismayed; we could not understand; we hoped;

our good-will would follow, and so on, and so on, as the orator warmed up to the occasion.

I could see Negro Joe and his family standing there, listening with a kind of dignified simplicity—taking every word in dead earnest. There they were in their little home, which, as we looked about it, seemed remarkably comfortable; as good a home as many a white family in the community lived in. They were evidently proud of it.

For some curious reason, we did not find the oration of our young lawyer so mirth-provoking as we had expected. Nor did he himself seem to find it so, although he finished with a grand peroration and presented the be-ribboned cane to "our admired fellow citizen whom we are about to lose—Mr. Joseph B. Blanton."

Some of us had never before heard his full name; he had always been "Negro Joe" or "Nigger Joe."

I shall never forget the picture of Joe standing there with the cane in his hand, or the way in which he stepped a little forward to respond.

"Gennelmen," he said, "I ain't never expect nothin' like this. I thank you, Mister

Cor'cran, for yo'r fine words. I thank you, gennelmen, for yo'r kin' thoughts."

He paused: you could have heard a pin drop in the room.

"Gennelmen, I respec' yo'; an' I thank yo'. There ain't never no trouble between folks that respec's each other—white or black. I express mah special gratitude to you, Mister Cor'cran, for all the fine words you say—an' for this gif' of yours which signifies yo'r respec'."

I recall how quietly we walked back into town, and how, just as we reached the corner, one of the boys broke out:

"Gosh! I never realised before that niggers were just like anybody else."

The very next day the sale notice came down from Joe's house, and the auction bill from the town hall—and we had the whole town laughing at us; it was months before poor Cochran heard the last of it.

In Tolstoi's books there are many fine passages regarding the wisdom, and often the happiness, of simple people: men who live close to the soil; or who through their lives have had to deal with disadvantages or hard conditions. He was thinking, of course, of the

Russian peasant; but I have been often reminded of it in talking with Negroes—which I greatly love to do.

Not long ago, since I have been here in the City, I had a talk by the merest chance with the Negro woman who takes care of the printer's office where I go every week. I had been detained later than usual, and she had come in to dust off the desks and chairs. I fell to talking with her. She was originally from Maryland; and she was a Roman Catholic—though most of our Negroes hereabouts are ardent Baptists or Methodists. There was something smiling and happy about her, even in the tones of her voice. She had been a servant, doing menial work, all her life.

"You appear to be happy," I said.

"Oh, Ah'm happy. Nobody ain't happier than I am."

"You've got plenty of hard work," I said.

"Ah don' min' that."

"But what is it that makes you happy?" I asked.

She laughed as though this were an odd question.

"Oh," said she, "Ise got lots o' good frien's

—and it don' matter whether white or black."

I thought I would sound her a little on the problem of the colour line.

"Oh, that don't trouble me!" She laughed. "I know my place; an' I know who my frien's is."

(How many people, I thought, white and black, lack this wisdom; how few know their place!)

"An' this colour line," she continued, "don' make no trouble when people is frien's, white or black."

I remember once hearing a coloured man I know tell of an experience which well illustrates one of the differences between white and black. I speak of this man advisedly as "coloured," for no one looking at him would ever have thought him a Negro. A Spaniard, an Armenian, an Italian, perhaps, but not a Negro. And he had a good education, he had read far more widely than many a white man of his calling; and yet in Tennessee, where he had lived, he was classified, by the iron law of caste, as a Negro.

He told me of a curious expression among coloured people, which I had never heard before: "Goin' over to white." Negroes who are almost white can sometimes cut away from their Negro life, settle in a new town or state, where they are not known, and "go white."

"I tried it once, long ago," said my coloured friend.

"Didn't it work?" I asked.

His answer quite astonished me.

"No," said he, "I didn't like it. White people don't have as good a time as coloured folks. They're stiff and cold. They aren't sociable. They don't know how to laugh!"

I never before had this glimpse of my race!

Then he told me of his experience. Thinking his life as a coloured man too hard, too much restricted, it came to him one day that he was white enough to pass almost anywhere for a white man, especially in the North. So he acted upon the inspiration.

He went to Memphis and bought a first-class ticket on a Mississippi River boat to Cincinnati. No one suspected him of being coloured, or, if they suspected, gave him the benefit of the doubt. He sat at the table with white people, occupied the chairs with them on the deck. At first, he told me, he could scarcely restrain his exultation, but after a time he began to be somehow lonesome.

"It grew colder and colder," said he.

In the evening of the second day he sat on the upper deck, and as he looked over the railing he could see, down below, the Negro passengers and deckhands talking and laughing. After a time, as it grew darker, they began to sing—the inimitable Negro songs, with their lift and swing, their strange, wistful sadness.

"That finished me," said he. "I got up and went downstairs and took my place among them. I've been coloured ever since."

I have often reflected upon the curious inner problems of the Negro—especially the mulatto, who has two racial spirits at war within him. Life must have strange, deep questions for him, not known to us. I remember once hearing an eloquent coloured minister—he classified as Negro!—set forth his personal problem thus:

"My father's father was a Black Hawk Indian seven feet tall. My father's mother was an Irish woman. My mother's father was an American white man. Her mother was a full-blooded African woman. What am I?"

Once, long ago, I heard a story of Jefferson Davis, President of the Southern Confederacy, which may or may not be true: It happened

at Washington before the Civil War, while
Davis was a United States Senator. A young
friend was walking with him down Pennsyl-
vania Avenue. They met a number of
Negroes on their way, each of whom bowed or
lifted his hat to Mr. Davis—and Mr. Davis
returned the bow. His young friend finally
expressed his surprise that the senator from
Mississippi should take such pains in returning
the salutations of the Negroes.

"I cannot allow any Negro," said Senator
Davis, "to outdo me in courtesy."

What a fine, high thing was this! It de-
serves to be worn, like a jewel, in one's
thoughts.

(I went once to dinner in a rich and comfortable home. A Negro maid waited at
table. The discussion turned upon Negroes,
and much was said of their amusing igno-
rances, their pretences, even their evil. Afterward the hostess told me with surprise that
she found the Negro maid crying in the pan-
try. This has hurt me for years whenever I
have thought of it.)

I wonder sometimes if society—as we now
know it—is not based upon the assumption
that men will do their worst rather than their

best; that they will all be beasts if they are
not made afraid of instant clubbing.   And this
has made me dream often of some fair country
where society assumed that men would do their
best instead of their worst; a country in which
they had learned the great truth that we all
make our own people as we go along, fashion
them, much as God does, after our own image.

I should like to live in such a country—

In that far country, as I have visited it,
often and often, in my thought, the people are
not equal any more than they are with us:
neither are they of the same colour or race, or
religion, or education—or anything whatsoever—but they have struck upon a marvel-
lously simple device for making life more
beautiful and happier than it is with us.   It
is not yet perfect, as the wisest among their
inhabitants know well, but it serves.

And this is the secret of it: Those of the
population of the country who are well born,
or educated, or rich—knowing well that these
benefits came to them by chance of birth or
fortune, and that almost all the good things
they have are due not to their own labour but
to the vision and toil of men long dead (Jesus
and Socrates and Newton and Shakespeare

and Washington and Lincoln)—knowing all this, as I say, these well-born or educated or rich men, instead of demanding that all the poorer people, all those of a different race or colour or religion, be honest, courteous, virtuous, and industrious, begin by being honest, virtuous, and noble themselves; by having themselves the courtesy they demand of others. It is strange how excellently well this policy works in that country. . . .

This, of course, is a dream. . . .

IX

JONAS

*"He most doth bathe in bliss
That hath a quiet mind."*

I HAVE had a day of quiet enjoyment: an amusing, lazy, inconsequential, but utterly charming day. If I had tried for a year I could never have imagined such a train of oddly quiet events, or dreamed of such curious, interesting, simple human beings. When I came home and thought of it all, I said to myself:

"Here is a day in which nothing of any consequence has happened—but, lord!—how I have enjoyed it!"

But the more I thought of it, the more it seemed to me that everything of any real consequence had happened; for is there anything better in this world than to know real people, and to be able to enjoy, utterly and completely, an entire day?   Stevenson says somewhere in one of his books that if one could add together all the days, hours, minutes in a lifetime that were fully worth living, the sum would be only forty.   Forty days worth living out of a life! I've had many more than that already, but if only that were true I could say that in this day I have lived one fortieth of my life.

The day began quietly enough. It being Sunday morning, quite early, I went down the steps into the sunny street.   In the country, at such an hour, life is as much on the go as ever; one can hear the hens cackling in their runways, and the bees humming, and the cattle calling, and the birds singing, and perhaps the whistling of some early boy in the fields!   Oh, it is fine in the country of a sunny Sunday morning in May!

But in the city everything quiets down of a Sunday morning; and the streets are as deserted as those of Sidon or of Tyre; and the tall still houses have a strange look, and such sounds as there are—a boy crying a paper, the iron ring of the milk-man's wheels on the stones—echo and reëcho as in a cavern. But how sweet the sun looking over the house-tops, stealing in at the windows, warming a cat curled on the steps! How pleasant the new leaves on old fretted ivy along the walls; how charming the ailanthus trees here and there leaning out of alleys and areaways!

All this came over me as I stepped out lazily into the Sunday morning sunshine. Where is spring not lovable?

"What in all the world, in all the world, they say,
Is half so sweet, so sweet, is half so sweet as May?"

It is the orioles that sing this, so the truthful poet reports—did he not hear them singing it? And they sing it well in the country I know best, where there are tall elm trees with swaying branches for orioles to nest in. But even a stranger in a far city can feel something of that delight on a sunny May morning.

It is this way with me: When I begin to enjoy a time like this I wish there were someone I could take in with me. So it was, by a perfectly natural process, that I thought of the Jensens, and of Jensen's garden, which I had not seen for some time. And that brought upon me a wave of longing for growing things, and I thought I would go in and see how Jensen's miniature garden was progressing. I had come to have a real liking for the old man.

I found him in the little area-way back of the house, and to my surprise quite dressed up —as though going away. He was resting in the sun, which was just high enough now to reach down between the buildings opposite and touch his little box of radishes and lettuce, now quite luxuriantly growing. The precious "punkins," however, which had been planted far too early and were now glassed over by Jensen's careful hands, looked lank and spindling.

There Jensen sat resting in the sun, with a calm look on his fine old face. He had seen much of life, and suffered much, and thought much, and was tranquil.

"I see, Jensen," I said, "that you are sitting, like Jonah, in the shade of your gourd."

He looked up with a smile.

"Aren't you afraid that Nineveh will be destroyed before you get there?"

He took his big pipe slowly out of his mouth to reply; but at this point Mrs. Jensen came bustling out of the door. She was also dressed up, quite astonishingly, with a bonnet that even I—who have never in my life seen of my own accord more than two bonnets—could not help seeing. She looked grand.

"Ve go for a tour," said she. "Jonas, he iss bringing soon his flivver, and ve go riding. All day ve ride."

Her excitement was fine to see; and when I began to express my interest she led me into the kitchen and showed me the blankets, sofa pillows, lunch baskets and the like—enough for an Arctic expedition. One thing rapidly led to another, and before I knew it Harriet and I had been invited to go with them.

"No, no, no!" cried out Mrs. Jensen, "ve haf plenty, plenty. You shall go with us in Jonas's flivver. Ve have plenty lunch."

I glanced around at Jensen. He was saying nothing with such a look of inviting friendliness that I could not help accepting. I went up the stairs much excited by the prospect and quite prepared to meet difficulty in overcoming Harriet's scruples. Sunday! But to my surprise, Harriet scarcely made a single objection, and in a few minutes we were at the steps, ready to go.

Jonas had just arrived with the "flivver," which now stood still, trembling a little, and barking like a tired dog, with two or three tolerably loud barks, then a little weak one. Jonas immediately leaped out, threw up the hood, and went at the machinery head first, with the result that the barking presently became quite steady, though still somewhat weary.

"I don't dare stop her," said Jonas—this flivver was apparently of the feminine gender —"for she's hard to start up again."

Jonas was a stocky young fellow, with a round head and prominent blue eyes. In honour of the occasion he wore an unaccustomed white collar and red tie. He had oil on his hands.

"Where are we going, Jonas?" I asked.

"Goin' fer a ride," said Jonas.

"But where?"

"Anywhere," said Jonas.

Mrs. Jensen came hurrying out with baskets, blankets, cushions—Jensen quite helpless.

"Hurry, Ma," said Jonas.

"Vell, do I not hurry, Jonas? What you t'ink!"

I sat up in the front seat with Jonas; Har-

riet with Mr. and Mrs. Jensen behind. **The**
flivver shuddered a few times under us, barked
desperately, and then with a leap started off
down the street, Mrs. Jensen crying out, "Ve
go; ve are off!"

It was something to see Jonas sitting up
there at the wheel, eyes sternly fixed upon the
road and hands grasping the steering gear as
though he himself were pushing the car. We
darted around a corner, dodged a silent policeman, passed a truck at thirty miles an hour
and swung finally into a broad boulevard.

"Gee," said Jonas, "she runs fine to-day!"

I glanced around to see Harriet holding on
her hat—and all smiling broadly.

"It's a fine day for a trip like this," said I,
trying to start up a conversation.

"You bet," said Jonas.

"Everyone seems to be going out into the
country," I continued.

"Sure," said Jonas.

"Do you like the city, Jonas?"

"Yep," said Jonas.

"When I was a young man," I said, "we
used to want to go West and take up new land
or look for a mine."

"Nix fer me," said Jonas.

So we rolled along gaily upon that broad, smooth city pavement, the wind in our faces, and all about spring sunshine and more and more trees, grass, open spaces. It was most exhilarating.

We stopped presently at a roadside station for gas, Jonas stepping out like one of the lords of creation.

"Fill 'er up, Bill."

While Bill was fillin' 'er up she coughed asthmatically under us, shook as though with a chill, and then suddenly stopped.

"Ve stop," cried out Mrs. Jensen excitedly.

Like one accustomed to the mishaps of life, Jonas seized the crank and turned it vigorously. She wheezed. She snorted. Jonas ran around to choke her. She gave a despairing flop and swooned away. Again Jonas went at the crank, again running around to set the throttle. The perspiration started upon his face.

"Ve do not go!" cried out Mrs. Jensen.

"Hey there," said Bill, the gasman, "ye ain't goin' to take all day startin'. Other people want to get gas."

With that Jonas and Bill, one on each side, ran "her" down the street some distance, out of the way of traffic.

"Ve are stopped," remarked Mrs. Jensen.

I looked around at Jensen, and saw that philosopher getting out his china pipe, the solace of many a misery; and presently he was blowing off puffs of smoke, and looking about upon the spring morning with the utter placidity of contentment.

Jonas was now quite in his element. He stripped off his good coat, slipped on a jumper, spread a rug on the pavement, got out a package of instruments, threw up the hood, crawled under the car—and generally enjoyed himself.

Mrs. Jensen, who had at first observed these proceedings with some anxiety, now followed the motions of Jonas with upsurging pride.

"Jonas, he knows," she assured us, "he vill fix 'er."

So we sat there in the fine spring sunshine. The automobiles in the road had now become numerous and there was a jolly, almost holiday, air about the people in them. One or two shouted jokingly at Jonas as they passed, or smiled at our predicament.

"David," said Harriet excitedly, "there's a rose-breasted grosbeak."

"What, here in the City!"

Sure enough, there he was in an open lot near by. It seemed quite like home.

"And look at the dandelions blooming!"

"And there are actually lilacs not gone yet."

I had not seen Harriet so much excited before since we came to the City. These were old country friends she was greeting; and this bird was a country bird; and this grass country grass; and this sunshine country sunshine. A pleasant glow came in her face. Jensen's eyes looked at her and then at me. There was a kind of blessing in that look. Presently he took his pipe slowly out of his mouth and said:

"Ah, ve lofe the spring."

Jonas was a long time at his fixing, but now that we had begun to look about us at the glory of the day—and to see the fine people rolling by in their cars—we minded it not at all. Presently Jonas arose from the bowels of the flivver, a broad grin on his face, and smut on his nose.

"I got her," he remarked.

He turned triumphantly at the crank, and, sure enough, she responded instantly with a loud snort. It was as though some obstruc‹ tion had suddenly come up out of her throat, She snorted again and again, with a kind of vainglorious excitement. She shook all over; she seemed about to blow up and be done with it. Jonas ran around to the throttle; and then she settled down suddenly to a steady snort-snort-snort.

I wish you could have seen Jonas at that moment. There he stood, well blacked, both face and hands, hair sticking every way for Sunday, perspiration pouring down his face— but with such a look of pride and satisfaction as cannot be depicted.

"Ah, Jonas," said Mrs. Jensen, "he iss good vit engines. He knows engines. Every engine he can start."

So now we were on our way again, headed for the open country. We rolled along as easily as you please, twenty, twenty-five, thirty miles an hour. We skirted around a great limousine as though it were standing still, we darted over crossings, we swung around corners, holding on for our lives.

"Gee," said Jonas, "she runs fine."

"Jonas, Jonas," cried Mrs. Jensen, "you vill kill us; you go too fast."

"This ain't nothin'," responded Jonas, out of the corner of his mouth without looking around—and straightway speeded up.

"She can make fifty easy," said he.

I glanced around to see Jensen drawn down in his seat, hanging on with both hands, his hair flying in the wind——

At that there was a loud explosion, and Jonas, with his feet braced on the brakes, came to such a sudden stop as nearly to throw us out. He swung out of his seat and looked down.

"Yep, she's blowed out," he observed.

Sure enough, a rear tire, which had been old when Germany first declared war, was now flat. Jonas was not in the least irritated. Off came the coat again, on the jumper, and he began changing the tire. He seemed actually to enjoy these opportunities to exhibit his skill.

Well, as a result of several incidents of this sort, noon found us not in the country, where we were bound, but near the corner of a park already occupied by a good many people. A bandstand was there under the trees, but the band had not yet arrived.

"Ve stop here," exclaimed Jensen, in great delight. "Ve haf music."

"Ah, Jensen, he lofes music," said Mrs. Jensen. "Vell, ve vill stop."

It was well said, for the "flivver" had again swooned away; and Jonas, now looking like a blacksmith at the end of a hard day's labour, was again changing into his jumper. So we all got out and carried the blankets, cushions, and baskets to a pleasant spot under a tree some distance back in the park. It was not near enough to the bandstand to suit Mrs. Jensen, but it was none the less a charming place. Above were wide-spreading maple boughs with little openings to the sunny sky. As we looked about we could see many people sitting or lying on the grass, some reading the Sunday papers, some eating their lunch, some stretched out in utter comfort, sleeping.

Mrs. Jensen's ceremony of preparation was something to see. First she spread down newspapers on the grass; over these she put down her blankets, then in the middle a red tablecloth with a fringed border. The baskets she disposed at two corners where she herself was presently to sit like a Queen between them. She moved so fast that Harriet, who tried to help, was quite useless. Jensen went for a pail of water at the public fountain.

"Jonas, come now," she called presently, "lunch is ready."

Jonas, lying head first under the car, did not reply.

"Jonas, *Jonas*. Sooch a boy!"

After much further calling, Jonas proceeded to the fountain, washed his face and arms, while his mother stood waiting to hand him a towel, and came presently with hair sticking straight up and face exactly the colour of a ripe tomato.

"Gee," said he, "I got 'er goin'."

His mind was still on the flivver.

What a luncheon was that! I think I have rarely seen Harriet more interested as one after another of the strange things came out of the basket. The strangest of all were a blood sausage and a round red-coloured cheese— such as no inhabitant of Hempfield had ever seen from the beginning of time. When Harriet expressed her wonder, Mrs. Jensen at once became volubly explanatory as to how in her youth, in Denmark, she had herself made cheeses and blood sausage.

So, vividly explaining, she cut the great sausage and the cheese and passed the pickled

cabbage and the rye bread.   It had been a long
time since breakfast in our Tower, and riding
in the open air, especially exposed to the terrors and alarums of Jonas's flivver, was sharp-
ening to the appetite.   It was downright good,
Mrs. Jensen's lunch (although I observed that
Harriet somehow avoided the blood sausage).
We had hot coffee poured out of thermos bottles; and, finally, at the end, the veritable surprise of the day, ice cream from a little pail
packed in ice.

"Jonas," said Mrs. Jensen, "he lofes ice
cream."

Jonas not only loved ice cream but everything else.   I began soon to understand why
Mrs. Jensen's baskets were so capacious.
Dishes started in both directions toward Jonas
and stopped there.   If there was anything left,
Jonas ate it.   It was a spectacle, a perform-
ance, a work of art, to see Jonas eating his
lunch.   Jonas had nothing to say, scarcely anything to think; his whole being was focussed
upon the business of lunching.   I had a bril-
liant idea as I sat there (which I think worth
at least ten thousand dollars); and this was
to put Jonas on the stage each evening at eight
o'clock and let him have his dinner there.   It

would bring down the house! And as he ate, Jonas grew redder and redder—if that were possible—looked more and more comfortably stuffed.

Jonas was second man on a truck owned by a wholesale grocery house. His father had tried to teach him his own beautiful art of bookbinding.

"Why should a feller spend years learnin' to be a bookbinder," said Jonas, "when he can git as much right off? I can pull down more'n any bookbinder in the trade, an' I ain't got to work more'n eight hours a day."

It was incomprehensible to Jonas how his father sometimes forgot himself and worked overtime on a binding—and so was late to his dinner.

"He ain't on to Amurrica," said Jonas.

I had often talked with Jensen about his earlier life; and he told me how, as a boy, he had learned to repeat part of the Norse Sagas; the stories of Frithiof, of Thor and Wodin and the Frost Giants. He was full of old poetry; and yet with a kind of humour, too.

"I remember ven I came on the ship to New York," said he, "I stood on the deck tinkin' I

vas Columbus; and the first ting I looked for
in Broadvay vas Indians."

The heroes of Jonas were quite different:
Ty Cobb and Dempsey; and instead of the lore
of Thor and Wodin he had Mutt and Jeff and
the movies.

He had also an apt and ready pragmatic
philosophy. I once asked him how he dared
drive a great new truck the company had
bought when he had not yet learned how:

"Oh, you ain't got to know," said he,
"you've only got to put it over."

Toward the close of our meal the band began to play, the music coming pleasantly to
us through the trees. Jensen drew back
against the maple trunk, lighted his pipe, and
sat there placidly smoking. Jonas returned
to his blessed car, and although it stood on the
roaring and dusty street he drew himself together and went to sleep on the back seat.

But it was Mrs. Jensen who most attracted
my attention. She sat there on the grass, legs
straight before her, and busy worn hands resting at last palm upward in her lap. As the
music stole across the sunny spaces, a curious
rapt look came over her face; and a kind of

absorbed gaze of the eyes as though they were
turned in upon the vague but deep memories of
the peasantry of a hundred generations. I
had a curious sense that here was no Mrs. Jensen; here was Woman dreaming of the deep
things of life. . . .

So we all sat there in delightful restfulness
and contentment, each thinking the thoughts
that came up to him out of his own past.

This love of getting out into the open fields
and woods in the spring, the delicious warm
days, is truly one of the deepest instincts of
humankind. Deep, deep in the race it stirs;
deeper than civilisation, deeper far than any
superficial memory or experience. For what
endless generations before man was really man,
before he knew himself, has our race crept
out of the miserable caves, hovels, and burrows
of our winter hiding places to the warm and
sunny hillsides of spring—and with what
nameless joy. It is deep in us, this love in
spring of the open woods, the trees, the fields,
the marshes. It is native to our family!
Congenial to our blood!

So we sat there for a long time, saying little,
listening to the music, resting, in utter com-

fort.   Occasionally Jensen would take his pipe
out of his mouth to make an observation, which
usually required no response.   Once, after his
eyes had followed with lazy fascination the
swiftly rolling traffic in the road, he remarked:

"In the old country ve know where ve go;
but in deese country dey go joost the same vid-
out knowing."

After a time Mrs. Jensen began to stir and
presently looked around to see if Jonas was still
sleeping in the car.   He was; and would continue to do so, as we discovered, until well
shaken.   Suddenly, without any preface whatever, Mrs. Jensen remarked:

"Jonas, he should marry.   I say to him,
'Jonas, why do you not marry?'   'Who shall
I marry, Ma?' says he.   'Vell,' says I, 'there
is Mary Sorenson; she iss a good von; a good
vorker.'   'Talk sense, Ma,' says he, 'she makes
more'n I do.   She pulls down her little forty-
five a veek,' says he."

Jensen remarked:

"It iss America!"

At this Mrs. Jensen fully waked up and with
indignation exclaimed:

"Do they not marry in America?   Why do
you say to ever'ting, 'It iss America'?   I say

Jonas, he should marry. He iss grown up, he should marry."

"Vell, you tell him," responded Jensen indulgently.

"I do tell him; but he laughs. He laughs. It iss the same when I tell him about religion and God. He says, 'They ain't no God.' Sooch a boy!"

"It iss America," said Jensen placidly.

"Ach!" exclaimed Mrs. Jensen indignantly, and started up to her feet.

The music had now stopped and the shadows had begun to lengthen, but the park still echoed with pleasant voices. We could see young lovers, groups of children, boyish friends, families, drifting along the walks or across the wide green spaces.

"Isn't it a fine thing," said Harriet, "that these people who cannot live in the country have a chance to come to a park like this?"

Mrs. Jensen now began to gather up the baskets and blankets and carry them down to the car. Upon each visit she gave Jonas a poke.

"Jonas, get up. Ve go."

But Jonas, his head crooked down on the seat, continued to snore. To the last Jensen remained sitting calmly by the tree, until the excited Mrs. Jensen, like a frantic hen with contrary chickens, succeeded in getting Jonas awake and Jensen up.

At length we were all loaded in and Jonas sitting bareheaded at the wheel, quite triumphant at the ready way in which "she" had started off for home.

"I think she smells her oats," said I.

I shall not soon forget the fine ride home we had in the cool of the evening, rolling easily along with a light breeze in our faces and exhilaration in our hearts. The entire city seemed homeward bound and many a car was loaded with the spoil of the woods. For some reason Jonas's flivver seemed content, like old balky horses I have known, to make the return journey without a single protest, landing us quite safe at the foot of our Tower.

"Here ve are," said Mrs. Jensen.

Harriet and I tried to express our great appreciation, but Mrs. Jensen would scarcely let us.

"Ve haf a good day!" said she. "Ve do what ve like."

When I thanked Jonas, he said:

"You bet."

So it was that I thought to myself, that evening:

"Here is a day in which nothing of any consequence has happened—but, lord!—how I have enjoyed it."

As I copy out this account of our expedition with Jonas, now two years afterward, my mind goes back still warmly to that day in May. I like well to think of the Jensens and their garden—hopeful every spring, hopeless every fall. I think sometimes our gardens, like our poems, our books, our true noble deeds, are best in the dreaming. Jensen's "punkins" were. He saw them with an April imagination climbing far up the brick walls, to the glory and astonishment of the neighbourhood; the great yellow globes pendant from the vines and supported by his own cunning invention in little woven string hammocks. But in August! I remember the straggling, dusty vine, the pale, half-wilted blossoms which no bees came to fertilise, and one long green accidental nubbin of a pumpkin through which some boy among those windowed cliff dwellings had, with sling shot, driven a hole. But Jensen loved it and watered it and nursed it and trained it to the last. The City, after all, will have its way. And yet men are interesting, not because they succeed—either as poets or pumpkin raisers— but by virtue of the bravery of their vision, the power of their intent.

X

THE ADVENTURE OF THE
SHABBY MAN

ONE morning, I remember vividly, in that
City, as I was walking down to the
print-shop of my misery, I saw a shabby-
looking man standing on the corner near a
cigar store. It came to me with a warm thrill
of amused excitement—how do such things
come to a man?—that if I liked, if I had
enough imagination and ingenuity, I could
come to know that shabby man, know all about
him, know him in such a way that he would
like me and be glad to help me in whatever I
was trying to do.

I stopped at the curb some distance away to turn this amusing thought over in my mind.

"No doubt," said I to myself, "if I wanted to get to the President of the United States, or the Emperor of Japan, or Henry Ford, I could start with him as well as any one. For we get to great people only by way of little ones."

I glanced again at my Shabby Man. He seemed gloriously at leisure and was entirely unconscious of the designs I had upon him. I thought he would not be irritated if I interrupted his meditations.

"No doubt," said I to myself, pursuing my project with new amusement, "he would know the boss of the street gang, or the corner policeman, or perhaps even the local political leader, and would introduce me:

"Boss, this is Mr. Grayson, a friend o' mine."

Then, if I had the imagination and ingenuity I could so interest the Boss or the Leader (he might think I had a vote or two to turn his way) that he would introduce me to the Congressman of his district ("Jim"—he would call him Jim to let me know he was on the best of terms with him—"Jim, this is Grayson, a good feller and a friend o' mine"), and the Congressman, being under obligations to the Boss, and he under obligations to the Shabby Man, and the Shabby Man to me, what would be easier, if I went down to Washington (and still had enough imagination and ingenuity!), than to persuade the Congressman to take me to the White House and introduce me to the President? And if I could meet the President——

At this I turned to look again, quite hopefully, at the Shabby Man—and he had totally disappeared, probably stepped into the cigar store or slipped around the corner while I wasn't looking and so, just as I was there in the White House, about to shake hands with the President—"How are you, Mr. President?" —down fell my beautiful project in complete ruin. I felt as though I had lost a great opportunity. I had been cheated of my just prey.

Well, I went down the street laughing heartily at myself, and yet somehow enjoying this little unimportant incident. When I told Mr. Pitwell about it afterward, he roared with laughter.

"I still think," said I, "it is a good way to get to the Emperor or Henry Ford, and one of these days, you'll see! I'll try it."

I should not describe this absurd incident at all if it were not for the further adventure it soon led me into, the results of which I truly prize. For it was only a few days later that I again met the Shabby Man.

Not far from our Tower in the City, we are blessed with an open square or common, which sometimes at evening, when failing light has blurred the hard angularity of the buildings all about and dimmed the evidences of human use, has a sweetness that reminds me of the country.

It is cooler there than in hot city streets, for little breezes adventuring in from the sea of an evening, being off duty, stop to play in the tree-tops. At the centre of it there is a pool of water, which, if you look at it from the right angle (as one must often look at sorry things), will sometimes give you back the sky or the stars. It is fed from a fountain at one side with water spurting from the uplifted bronze beak of a swan held fast in the arms of a fat, naked, rusty bronze Cupid. Sometimes, just at evening, three Italians, two with violins and one with a piccolo, come there to play funny lively music, and afterward go about smiling broadly to collect a tariff of pennies. In the daytime this charming spot swarms with chil-

dren; but in the evening lovers meet there, and
old men sit in the seats to rest, and sometimes
an orator comes to the street-side to tell the
populace how the evils of this crooked universe
of ours can be quickly cured by taking his
particular pill.

I have loved to walk in this small common
and look at all the people who are there, all
the strange, poor, fascinating, valuable people.
I had also another secret purpose which, now
that the danger is past, I may openly disclose.
I discovered to my amazement one day that a
pair of our own familiar song-sparrows—that
cheerfulest of birds—was actually nesting in
a low thicket of viburnum and hemlocks near
one corner of the common.

All about, day by day, played the children,
the City clanged and roared, and all night long
blazed the lights of the streets—and yet these
birds tranquilly nested there. I cannot tell the
delight I had in finding their nest, nor the
curious sense of kinship I felt for other wild
things caught in the City (and making the best
of it). I made many an anxious, tiptoeing
visit to see how the family progressed—I had
to be shy, I can tell you, with sharp-eyed boys
about; or with my back turned as innocent

as you please, I listened to the exquisite low music of the male bird as he hid near the nest.

I suppose I ought not to interrupt the current of my story for so long a description of the little common; but somehow I love it, and cannot let it go by without a word or two. For how can any little pleasant place be all it should to us unless we say truly what we feel about it?

It was here, one evening, that I saw again the Shabby Man who had set me on my absurd imaginings. He was taking his ease, as it were, in his own pleasant garden, looking about him quite tranquilly. No millionaire in his own private park could have seemed more complacent. I saw him some distance away and decided with a thrill that this time he should not escape me.

Yet I was in no hurry. I even stopped a moment to consider, with eager amusement, how I should go about capturing him. I had an idea that I should like to find out why he was shabby.

As I have already related, I have had much joy in certain amusing adventures, playing country Caliph visiting incognito this dim Bag-

dad of a City.   Should I try being Caliph with
the Shabby Man?

I decided instantly in the negative.   In fact,
I had begun to grow rather tired of that
method.   While I had had a thundering success with it—or so I considered it—when I met
Mr. Pitwell, the later adventures had been
checkered.   The business decidedly had its ups
and downs.

You see, while I was thinking of myself as a
Caliph, other people, looking me over, did not,
somehow, get any such idea.   I knew well what
I was inside, but they didn't.   They were conscious only of a rather awkward country-
looking man interrupting them while they were
busy with pick and shovel digging for gold; and
since he could contribute no practical hints to
help them with their digging, and because they
were always a little suspicious lest, while he
fixed them with his glittering eye, he would
cunningly make away with some of the nuggets
they turned up, they sometimes made short
work of him.

It came over me, then, in a flash of amusement, how I would do it.

"I will be a kind of Socrates of this Athens,"
I said, "and floor him with questions."

I liked the idea tremendously. As to the
method itself, it was old enough—had I not
asked Yankee questions, recklessly and gloriously for years in the country?   But the sudden feeling that I could myself be the veritable
Socrates of this task (I actually felt of my nose
to see whether it would qualify in socratic stub-
biness), was boundlessly delightful.   Socrates
immediately and completely elbowed the Caliph
off the scene (being no doubt a stronger character).

So it was that Socrates strolled along the
street of Athens.   Over there was the Parthe-
non; and this, though the identification was not
complete, was the agora.   It was evening in
Athens.

"How are you?" said Socrates to the Shabby
Man.

"How are *you*?" said the Shabby Man to
Socrates.

He moved along a little in an inviting way—
being no doubt glad of any interruption—and
Socrates sat down on the bench beside him.

"I see," said Socrates, "that you are taking
your ease in your garden."

It is the way of Socrates to begin anywhere.

"*My* garden," said the Shabby Man some-

what indignantly; "where did you git that
idee?"

"Are you not sitting here freely, of your own
will?"

"Why, yes," said the Shabby Man; "they
ain't nobody compellin' me."

"And can any one, by any law, make you
move?"

"No," said the Shabby Man.

"Do you think any millionaire who sat here
could have any pleasanter views or cooler airs
than you have now?"

"Why, no," said the Shabby Man; "but, dang
it, what are ye drivin' at?"

"Well, then," said Socrates calmly, "I have
proved, haven't I, that this is your garden—at
least, as much yours as any one's?"

I wish you could have seen the expression on
the Shabby Man's face. Socrates in his own
day must have had no end of inner amusement.
But the Shabby Man, lingering on corners or
sitting on park benches, had also seen something of human nature.

"Say, neighbour," said he, "I ain't particular,
but are you all straight?" And he tapped his
forehead with one finger.

"You have not answered my question," said

Socrates—you will remember that Socrates never allowed his victims to wriggle away from him. "Isn't this your garden you are sitting in?"

"Say, this here is a public park."

So literalism, like an incubus, sits upon the soul of man!

"I see plainly," said Socrates, "that you do not know how rich you really are. Did you ever think that whatever you can enjoy belongs to you?"

The question missed the Shabby Man entirely, but he pounced like a hawk upon the assumption that he was rich without knowing it.

"Me—rich!" he exclaimed, showing at last some real heat. "Rich!"

"I feel certain," remarked Socrates, "that you didn't know it, else you would be a happy man to-night."

(I liked being Socrates better the further I got along with it.)

The Shabby Man edged a little away, and glanced down as though he expected to find his pockets suddenly full of money:

"Say, neighbour, what do you mean?"

"Isn't this open space here in the crowded city valuable?"

"Why, yes," said the Shabby Man; "course it is."

"And these trees—and fine walks and seats —and that fountain playing there, aren't they precious? Aren't they costly? Aren't they beautiful?"

The Shabby Man was beginning plainly to be angry; but Socrates did not wait, this time, for an answer, but, leaning over a little nearer, put another question.

"Did you ever think of the men who are at work the year round, or of the money that citizens contribute, to make a pleasant place like this where you and I can come and sit in the evening and enjoy ourselves?"

"Huh!" said the Shabby Man. "You mean these here lazy white-wings that rake up the leaves in the park! A lot o' grafters, I say! I know 'em. And I know the man that bosses 'em. He couldn't make a livin' poundin' sand in a rat hole. I *know* 'em."

"That's the very trouble!" said Socrates. "Isn't it odd how much annoyance we rich ones, we aristocrats, have with our servants? We can't sit at ease of an evening in our own garden and enjoy the beauty or the quiet of it, can we? without thinking of the indecent neglect of those who work for us?"

I don't know that I blame the Shabby Man for being restless and even angry; no one likes to be driven into a hole with questions. I don't wonder that Socrates, back there in old Greece, had finally to drink the hemlock. He must have been a truly uncomfortable character. Down with him! And I don't know what might have happened next if there had not been an interruption which provided an easy way for the Shabby Man to escape.

This interruption was the orator I have already mentioned, who came of pleasant evenings to discourse to the multitudes (he had often as many as twenty or thirty people to listen to him) upon the state of the nation and the world. He had a curious wooden chair which he brought with him. It had a straight high back with a box attached to it, wherein he kept pamphlets for sale. He would plant this chair upon the pavement, mount upon the seat, take off his hat and run his fingers through his sleek black hair, and begin with a voice that would put to shame the bull of Bashan:

"The man had the passionate sincerity of one who had him-self suffered."

"Fellow citizens."

It was he who interrupted our Socratic dia-
logue there in the park. The Shabby Man
drifted into his audience. I had myself seen
him a number of times and had even stopped
to listen to him; but I had never looked upon
him save as a picturesque feature of the life of
the City.

But that night I was stirred by my adventure
with the Shabby Man, and wondered what it
was in this orator that drew him away. So I
also joined in the audience. I felt far from being satisfied with my pursuit of the Shabby
Man which I had begun so jauntily. I had not
captured him, much less found out why he was
shabby. I hated to let him get away from me.

Well, I listened intently to the orator until he
had finished this speech, and I listened to the
discussion that followed.

It was a remarkable talk. The man had the
passionate sincerity of one who had himself
suffered. He had been a journeyman printer,
and in the course of a hard life had learned not
only to read his galleys upside down, as printers
do, but everything else under the sun. Half
the world judges the other half by its hurts.

Well, he gave appealing or humorous

glimpses of his experiences, so that I thought I should like to know much more about him, and I felt envious of the power he had of stirring up the men who gathered around him.

His whole message could be boiled down into a few sentences: He told his hearers that they were poor and having a hard time of it, that they were not getting half what was rightly theirs, and that the fault lay in the Government, in the laws, in society as it was organised. His advice to these men was to demand their rights and step up and take what was their own.

I think this a fair statement of the essence of his message; and one hearing it honestly could not deny that there was much truth in what the man said. When has power ever been just with weakness? His hearers literally drank up his words. They were flattered to learn that they were having a hard time and were not getting enough pay—and that the trouble was not with them but with other people or with a distant government.

These thoughts came whirling upon me as I walked away after the orator had finished, and I was so absorbed that I forgot the existence of the Shabby Man and the playful mood of the earlier evening. For when a man gets a glimpse of even a partial truth passionately expressed, he must make a place for it in his thinking, or it will continue to plague him.

"I expect," I said to myself, "I have too much of the countryman in me to wish to be pitied for anything whatsoever; and, so far from having a hard time of it, it seems to me I have had, always, far more out of life than I myself earned. And when I think of my troubles, it seems to me I have caused most of them myself."

It came over me suddenly and humorously and I said to myself:

"One of these nights I will bring *my* soap box and get up there by that orator, and every time that he tells the people how poor they are and how much society owes them, I'll tell 'em how rich they are, and how much they owe society."

This picture immensely struck my fancy.

"Between us," I said, "we'll manage to get out the whole truth; but"—and I saw the consequences with startling vividness,—"I'll be the one to be knocked on the head. No one in these days wants to be reminded that he owes anything."

I was so absorbed in these amusing speculations that I was startled when I felt someone touch me on the arm. I glanced around. It was the Shabby Man walking beside me. An indescribable change had come over his face. Earlier in the evening he had seemed cowed and on the defensive. Now he looked bold.

"Say, neighbour," said he, "what did you think o' the speech? Had the goods, eh!"

I could see that the Shabby Man had been stirred.

"Well," said I, "there was much truth in what he said."

"I'm tellin' ye," said the Shabby Man enthusiastically.

"He made a pretty good story about what society owes men like you and me now, didn't he?"

"You bet he did," said the Shabby Man.

(I did not recall until afterward that in all the conversation that followed I never once thought of being Socrates!)

"If I had all that was comin' to me," continued the Shabby Man before I could reply, "I wouldn't be here."

"Where would you be?" I asked.

"Well, I'd be—I don't know exactly where I'd be, only, I wouldn't be here."

"What's wrong with it here?" I asked.

"A man can't be a man in this hole of a place. It's a prison, that's what it is."

"That's curious," said I, "I knew a man once who was in prison, but he had that in him which made him happy there. Whenever I went to see him he made it seem better to be in prison than it was outside."

The Shabby Man looked puzzled; his face fell.

"There you go again," said he, "arguin'."

I laughed.

"Let's sit down a moment," said I, "it isn't late. We were both interested in that speech——"

"You bet!" he interrupted.

"And we can talk about it."

So we sat down on a nearby bench.

"Did you ever," said I, "look at that library over on the corner?"

"Sure; been in it, too."

"And see the names they've got up there cut in the stone?"

"Sure."

"Newton and Franklin and Lincoln and Shakespeare and Cervantes and Milton, and so on?"

"Sure, I've seen 'em."

"How do they make you feel?"

"Why, I don't know's I feel anything in particular. How do you feel?"

I laughed.

"You'll smile when I tell you," I said, "but I never go along there without wanting to take off my hat to them. Thank you, Ben Franklin, for flying a kite in a thunderstorm; it has meant a lot to me since. Thank you, Edison, for the electric lamp; I could hardly live without it. And I always make an especially low bow to Abe Lincoln, for I don't know of any man in this world who did more good without getting in his own way than Abe Lincoln. When I consider sometimes what has been done for me by the great men of the past—often done with much sorrow and suffering—I feel as though I were a deeply indebted man. I have been surrounded by incalculable benefits and luxuries, like this pleasant park, which I did nothing to earn and can never hope to pay for."

I'll have to be honest; my Shabby Man looked dazed, as though he did not at all understand what I was driving at.

"Say," he said after a pause, "I thought we was goin' to talk about that speech."

"All right," said I, "let's talk about it. That

orator made us feel that we were pretty badly
treated, that we weren't getting what was coming to us."

"Sure, and it's right too."

"I suppose a large part of the people in this
city feel that they are being abused and not
getting all they ought to."

"You bet there's a lot o' discontent, and,
what's more, we're goin' to do something about
it."

"Should you say that there were as many as
ninety out of every hundred people who feel
that way?"

"Ninety-nine anyway," said the Shabby
Man.

"You might," said I, "call it a kind of universal creditor frame of mind. Everybody
believes that other people owe him and he owes
nobody."

The Shabby Man looked still more puzzled
and began to appear uneasy.

"Now you're arguin' again," said he.

"But," said I, "it's an intensely interesting
problem to me.   If ninety-nine men feel themselves creditors and only one recognises that he
owes anything, how is the one going to satisfy
the ninety-nine?"

I could see now that I had entirely lost the Shabby Man. The exhilaration he had shown after the speech had gradually faded away and he was back where he was when I found him. You can easily steer a ship that is going somewhere, but how steer a ship that is shoaled?

After we parted I walked the dark streets of the city for an hour, thinking hotly of all I had seen and heard that night. As I was going up the dim stairway to our Tower the whole affair seemed to come suddenly clear to me, so that I stopped there on the landing and laughed aloud.

"Human beings are curious," I said, "curious and contradictory, but amazingly interesting."

"Where *have* you been?" asked Harriet when I came in.

"Harriet," said I, "I have made a great discovery about this world."

Harriet said nothing. I expect she is accustomed by now to my great discoveries.

"All times are great," I said, "exactly in proportion as men feel, profoundly, their indebtedness to something or other; to the gods with the Greeks; to Jehovah with the Jews; to Jesus with Christians; to science with many a modern. A feeling of immeasurable obligation puts life into a man, and fight into him, and joy into him. A sense of profound indebtedness makes a man beautiful."

I paused.

"And," said I, "when a man thinks everybody owes him and he owes nobody, he soon grows—well, shabby."

In the night I woke up with the somewhat uncomfortable feeling that I had been orating again, when I keep saying to myself that it is enough to understand. (No one ought to orate!) But presently I turned over:

"It's what I actually thought. It's the kind of man I am. If I tried being anything different, or saying anything different, I'd fail."

So I turned over and went comfortably to sleep again.

XI

THE MAN AFRAID

ONE of the greatest pleasures I have had
since I began writing these "Adventures," now many years ago, has been the letters I have received. But some have had in
them, so it seemed to me, a strange background
of tragedy; for these writers, contrary to the
common report concerning what men want
most, seek something that no money, no position in life, no law, not even any institution,
can satisfy. They cannot find rest in dollars.

So it is that I have concluded from these letters, and from much other experience of life,
that the chief thing desired in this world by
human beings is a working agreement of a man
with himself; that is, unity or peace within.
If a man have that—if he can live upon
friendly terms with himself—nothing else
seems to matter.

For lack of this agreement within, the place
of which is taken by tumultuous civil war, each
man fighting himself, most human beings are
sad.

I was thinking some such things as these the
other day when walking the streets of the City,
where there is much strife and little tranquil-
lity, and came home to my Tower to find a
letter addressed to me from a stranger. It
was a curious letter, which made me feel at
once that it was written by a man who was
afraid of life. It was not that he said in so
many words, "I am afraid," but he put in fear
as he would put in a comma at each pause in
the sentences, and fear lurked, like a period, at
the end of it.

I read over this letter several times, for there
was true feeling in it, and finally looked up and
said to Harriet:

"There is nothing that comes to a man so dreadful as fear."

"That," said Harriet, "is true."

"And fear of life," said I, "is worse than fear of death."

"That is also true," said Harriet.

The man's name was Thorpe; and I could not get him out of my mind.

"This man Thorpe," said I to myself, "feels strongly and suffers deeply."

Two or three times I sat down to answer his letter, thinking I would put courage, like commas, in my reply, and hope, like a period, at the end of it. But I have been long a writer and know well the poverty of the written word. Language, at best, is a poor method of conveying what one truly feels. There will perhaps come a time when thought, leaping clear of the slow wires of language, will cross boundless space when one soul tunes to the wavelength of another.

I could not make my letter to this man Thorpe convey what I felt. As I read again what he said it seemed to me that he had much fineness of spirit—hidden fineness, easily hurt —covered and concealed by the kind of whis-

tling which is supposed to keep the courage up.
He would be a man who would shrink from
rough contacts, and by virtue of the gentleness
of his nature would suffer not only for himself
but even more keenly for those he loved.   For
to love—if a man have not come to understanding—is to suffer; and the deeper the love the
sharper the suffering.   I know this.

His letter gave little evidence of his outward
circumstances, save that it indicated a good
background of cultivation.

"He is probably a poor man," said I to myself, "say, an unsuccessful professional man,
or a teacher, or an artist, who is afraid for
himself and his family because he is poor.
Poverty is a skilful intimidator."

This was the way I pictured him: a harried
and worn human being living in some teeming
hive of an apartment, cut off from pleasant and
comforting scenes and being crowded slowly to
death by the cares of life.   (A mere leaf of
grass will hold up a cobweb.)

"Why," asked Harriet, "do you talk so much
about this Mr. Thorpe—whom you have never
seen?"

Harriet is a sensible person.

"Harriet," said I, "human beings are inconceivably interesting, and how can you know them without thinking about them?"

"Well," said Harriet, "you can easily satisfy your interest; you can go and see this Mr. Thorpe.   He lives in this city."

This suggestion came to me with the shock of discovery.

"So I can."

I suppose I am stupid, but I had been so absorbed in picturing this Mr. Thorpe as a kind of abstraction—the man afraid—that I had not thought of going any farther.   And he might be living in the next street or so.   It came upon me with a warm glow.

"I'll go now," said I, jumping up and reaching for my hat.

"David!"

When Harriet speaks in that tone I know something is wrong.

"It's ten o'clock at night," said she.

"So it is," I said.   "I'll go to-morrow."

I expect you will think me ridiculous to become so excited over a matter like this, but so it was.   It seemed to me such a chance as I had never had before to test out my thoughts

regarding such a character as I conceived this
Mr. Thorpe to be, with the man Thorpe himself, the reality. I lay awake that night picturing to myself all the various strange,
unexpected, amusing, even shocking things that
might happen. I soon had two or three first-
class stories about Mr. Thorpe growing like
mushrooms in my imagination—each leading
away to a different conclusion but all strung
upon the red thread of fear. (The difference
between a story and true life is that the first
must have an ending, while the second goes
straight on to the stars.)

The quite simple rush of sympathy I had felt
when I first read this man Thorpe's letter was
losing itself in a maze of speculation. I could
feel myself rapidly becoming a mere story-
smith, forgetting that this was a live man, loving, suffering and afraid.

There is something cold and hard about
daylight in a city, and great bare stone buildings, and cars pounding through the streets,
and boys crying the afternoon papers; and
when I turned in at the address given upon
Mr. Thorpe's letter—it was an office building
of the older sort, yet prosperous-looking—I
had a strange shrinking feeling. I hesitated

inside the door and for an instant the whole
project seemed absurdly quixotic.   Why should
I bother this man Thorpe?   I would probably
be disappointed in him and he in me, for we
would see only the outsides of each other.   And
then the thought of the man himself as he had
wonderfully expressed himself in his letter
came over me warmly, and I said aloud:

"I must see this Mr. Thorpe."

I suppose surprise is of the essence of adventure, and what, after all, is more surprising than reality?   I had to laugh at myself, so
feeble did all my imaginings appear.   Instead
of the shabby apartments I had so vividly
pictured in my mind—where the worn Mr.
Thorpe ate out his heart with fear—I stepped
into a roomy office which exhaled the veritable aroma of prosperity.   I can think of no
one word that conveys the essential impression
it gave as well as "metallic."   All the furniture seemed made of hard metal, sharp corners,
and glittering surfaces.   The typewriters had
a biting metallic click and the heels of the hurrying clerks upon the hard floor sent out a metallic
echo.   The voice of the girl at the telephone
seemed to be made out of the wires of her in-
strument, so hard, sharp, cut-off, it was.

Everything was running like a perfectly oiled machine, so that I thought that if a man were to live long in such a place his brain would begin to tick like a clock.

At first I said to myself, "Mr. Thorpe is undoubtedly a poor bookkeeper, or a stockman, or some little caged secretary, afraid of his life." But I discovered immediately that Mr. Thorpe was none other than the manager, the superior, the veritable king of the place. It was *his* office. His name in large letters was there on an inner door.

"It is going to be more exciting than I thought," I said to myself.

I cannot describe the eagerness I now felt to see, actually see, the kind of outer man who would cover such a spirit as I had found in Mr. Thorpe's letter.

It appeared immediately that Mr. Thorpe was hard to get at, very much engaged and so forth. The Cerberus at the gate was delightful enough—she had indeed, only one head, and a very pretty one it was, but it served as well as three.

"Is your business urgent?" she asked.

"Most urgent," said I.

"Are you—selling something?"

You can see what skepticism prevails among the young!

"No," said I, "I am giving it away."

I looked at her and smiled.

"Oh," said she.

"But," I said, "what I give away many people would be glad to buy."

This remark seemed to confirm her worst suspicions. I could see exactly what was going on behind her bright eyes.

"You think I am odd, don't you?"

"Well——"

"And you think I am trying to get to Mr. Thorpe to sell him some bonds, or books, or a patent warming pad?"

"Well——" she was smiling broadly.

"You tell Mr. Thorpe that there is an odd sort of man out here—you can describe me with as much humour as you like, it won't hurt me—and that he wants to see me. Tell him he wrote this man a fine letter—a personal letter —on June 16th. Tell him this man's name is Grayson."

Human nature is curious. I had thought that after writing me such an appealing letter Mr. Thorpe would receive me with open arms. But, as I reflected afterward, I should have

known better, for the essence of the man was
fear. He could impulsively pour out his
harried soul in a letter to an unknown writer
who had touched him; but when that writer
appeared upon the scene, an actual, common
person (probably quite different from what he
expected), he scurried away within himself and
shrank from the contact. The shells of human
beings cause most of the trouble in this world!
They not only keep other people out but they
keep the man himself in.

I found him standing quite forbiddingly behind his desk—a rather large, though active
man, with dark eyes. He was immaculately
dressed and wore to perfection the easy mask
of One Weary with Large Concerns. He
seemed at first sight positively repelling.

For an instant I would have given half I
possessed if I had not come: the difficulty of
reaching any simple human relationship—and
that was all I cared for—seemed insuperable.
I groped for the right word to say, but it would
not come. I heard the door close behind me,
as the secretary went out, and had a momen-
tary feeling of panic, as though I were caught
there, in a trap. I looked helplessly at Mr.
Thorpe and he looked helplessly at me. If

there had not been that strange letter, that spark of the spirit, between us, he would probably have given me a business-like "Bow-wow," and I should have replied "Bow, wow, wow," and we would have parted upon the open road of the world.

Suddenly, like a flash, I seemed to come around a corner and catch a glimpse of the ridiculous picture we made. There I stood awkwardly, hat in hand, in the middle of this chilly office, on the absurdest, most quixotic errand one could imagine—and with nothing whatever to say. What a fool was I!

Well, I burst out laughing. I could not help it. At which Mr. Thorpe seemed still more to shrink into himself, grow more erect and repellent. But I was now determined to carry it through.

"I hope you will pardon me for laughing," I said, "but it came over me all at once what a terribly dangerous thing it is to write a book. It gets a man into the most ridiculous situations."

Mr. Thorpe stirred restlessly, but still said nothing.

"I write a book," said I, "and aim it at no one in particular. I shoot it off with my eyes closed. It hits you. You write me a letter which, in return, hits me. I think a good deal about that letter, and try to answer it and cannot; but I say to myself, 'This Mr. Thorpe is a man I should like to know.' So I begin to consider what kind of a man you are, what you do and how you live. And by a kind of magic we are together! You can easily see what a dangerous thing it is to write a book."

In my eagerness I had stepped up close to his desk and found myself leaning over it toward him. I was tremendously excited, and yet somehow amused. I thought I could see his countenance changing, and went on eagerly:

"You'd laugh too if you could know how I pictured you."

With that I gave him a graphic and humorous description of some of my absurd speculations about him, based upon his own letter.

"And there you were, living miserably in a crowded tenement, cut off from pleasant and comforting things—and poor, oh, very poor."

I could see all along that Mr. Thorpe was having difficulty in maintaining his composure, and at this last remark he laughed outright.

"And you got all that out of my letter!" he exclaimed.

"Oh, that was only the bare beginning of it. I could a tale unfold——"

"And I was poor?"

"Very poor."

"Why did my letter make you think I was poor?"

"Because you were so afraid of life."

This remark had the most surprising effect upon Mr. Thorpe. I have thought since that if I had been trying to imagine such a scene I should never have conceived a transformation so swift. He started, and the blood quite left his face. He dropped down into his chair, all the imposing dignity of his former pose suddenly disappearing. Leaning over the corner of his desk toward me, he said sharply:

"I never said I was afraid of any one or anything."

His voice had taken on a new intensity.

"No, you did not actually say it in so many words," I replied; "but you made me feel it. I knew it as well as though you had spent a week telling me."

"I made you feel that! I never thought I'd admit such a thing to any man; I hardly admit it to myself."

He paused. If ever the bare suffering soul of any man came into his eyes, Thorpe's came at that moment.

"But it's true," said he, "it's true. I happened on something in your book that somehow made me think you would understand, and on the spur of the moment I wrote you that letter."

"And regretted it afterward," I said.

"How did you know that?"

"Don't think I haven't been all through it myself."

"You have!" he exclaimed eagerly.

We had unconsciously been drawing closer and closer together until we were now sitting opposite each other. I could put my hand on his knee.

"Afraid!" said I. "I've been afraid of more ridiculous things than you ever have—I'll bet. One of the things I was once afraid to do was to let out all that I was—my ignorance, envy, ingenuousness, egotism, to say nothing of far worse follies. You see, we all want to appear something other than we are. We'd rather appear worse than we are (there is a kind of superiority in a reputation for devilishness) than actually what we are. But one day I found out what a joke I was playing on my-self."

"What do you mean—a joke?"

"Why, I saw all at once that a man cannot possibly conceal himself or appear either better or worse than he is, not for long! for the secret leaks out at every look. There is no style, no art, no lie, that can long cover up what a man is. It discloses itself in every word he says, every line he writes—whether he will or no— and gets itself soon published abroad. This may be clear enough to many men; but long ago it came to me as a kind of discovery. It made me laugh at myself and that ended my fear."

"It did!" he exclaimed eagerly.

"Yes," said I, "to be able to laugh at one's self is the beginning of peace—and you cannot imagine the comfort I began to feel. The sense of wishing to be known only for what one really is is like putting on an old, easy, comfort-able garment. You are no longer afraid of anybody or anything. You say to yourself, 'Here I am—just so ugly, dull, poor, beautiful, rich, interesting, amusing, ridiculous—take me or leave me.'

"And how absolutely beautiful it is to be do-ing only what lies within your own capacities and is part of your own nature. It is like a great burden rolled off a man's back when he comes to want to appear nothing that he is not, to take out of life only what is truly his own, and to wait for something strong and deep within him or behind him to work through him."

Afterward, when I thought of it, I was ashamed that I should have said so much, and in such a way, at the very start, but so it was. But it is possible that my own frankness stimulated his. At any rate, the next hour was truly one of the most remarkable I ever spent. I think the man was literally starving in his spirit to talk with someone who could, in some degree, understand. (We have no institution in our roaring modern life that quite fills the place of the old confessional.) He had been fighting a civil war within himself until he was exhausted.

Well, the man literally poured himself out, struggling for words with which the more mercilessly to expose himself. The telephone rang, but he did not hear it. The door opened and a secretary tiptoed in. He looked up and said:

"I'm not to be called up. I cannot see any-body."

"It isn't that I'm afraid of death," he went on, "I think sometimes death would be an easy way out.   Life is what has been too much for me."

I shall not attempt here to put down the entire story he told, it would make a small book, but I think I can give the essence of it in a few paragraphs.

He said that what he wanted was to feel safe, secure, and he could not.   It was not for himself alone that he wanted to feel secure, but still more for his wife and his children.   He said that he tried to reason about it but continued to worry.   It was plain that he was a man of deep affections, especially for his children, and curiously for his old father.   All that he wanted, he said, was money enough to meet the contingencies of life; but he could not be sure either that he had it or could ever get it.

"You'll probably smile when I tell you," said he, "but I'm positively obsessed about insurance.   I suppose it's an indication of my state of mind.   I've insured against everything I can think of: fire, accidents, disease, robbery, death—but the more I insure the more fearful I seem to grow that something will happen, some scurvy trick, that will wipe me out."

It was strange to me how clearly he saw his own condition and yet could not deal with it.

It was the same regarding his health and that of his family. He had sought out the best doctors in the country and even in Europe: doctors, hygienists, posturists, food specialists, and even those strange, new men who pretend to cure the mind—hoping by science to reduce the hazards of life; but the more doctors he had, the more fearful he grew that some unsuspected weakness or disease would leap out upon him.

He told me that he had had the best possible sort of upbringing. His father was a preacher, "a great preacher," he said, "of the old sort." What his father preached was fear. He frightened people with the terrors both of life and of death, and so tried to drive them to thoughts of God. He succeeded in thoroughly frightening his own son, for the son accepted the idea of the danger of life without adopting the dogma that was to relieve it. The old man, still himself living, mourned over his son, whose sufferings he blindly felt but did not understand.

Thorpe's wife! He told me also about her, for, once started, he would stop at nothing. She was brought up accustomed to every sort of material convenience and comfort. She was evidently the kind that could be satisfied only with ample means. She did not fear life—only poverty. Thorpe loved her deeply and, when unirritated by not having everything she wanted, she was plainly an agreeable and lovable woman. But how she added to Thorpe's fears, how she crucified him with daily alarms lest he be unable to satisfy her requirements of house, clothing, position. And his fear was not content with dwelling upon present difficulties and dangers, but raced wildly into the future, and pictured the cruelty of life a year, ten years, even two generations away.

All this may seem extravagant, but it is what he told me.

Thorpe's children!

"Well," said he, "you might think I could feel sure about them; but I see clearly that what we are doing is to train them, also, daily and hourly, in being afraid of everything under the sun: physical, intellectual, social, moral. What chance have they of not finding life too much for them?"

Of course Thorpe was an intense conservative in all things: politics, religion, business, education (for fear is the backbone of conservatism). There seemed greater safety in that which was settled, tried out, established! All change, experiment, adventure, was a terror to him, a leap in the dark. He loathed books or plays that bit down on life; he sought diversion and anodynes.

It seemed to me as the man talked, and I listened, never interrupting, that one who thus fears life dies a thousand deaths. The wise accept the chances of life and go forward joyfully.

He finished with a helpless wave of his hand and sat back in his chair. I had been trying for some time to think what I could say that would help, but in the presence of such a catastrophe what *can* one say?

I must have been silent longer than I supposed, for Mr. Thorpe said finally:

"What do you make out of a miserable story like that? It makes you smile, doesn't it?"

"Was I smiling?" I said. "It wasn't at that; it wasn't at anything you said. But while you were talking, especially there at the last, I could not help thinking of a man I knew when I was a boy. He was one of the great unknown men—to me, at least. As you were talking he seemed trying to get out of me and say something: that is one of the ways he has of taking his immortality—talking through me —and he is urgent about it. Would you care to hear about him?"

Mr. Thorpe waved his hand in the way of the man whose troubles are so great that nothing any more matters.

"I never think of him," said I, "without a peculiar feeling of comfort. To this day the picture of him I have in my mind makes me smile. He was a German, an old German. There was always something of a mystery about him, in the gossipy Western town where I grew up. He came to America just after the Franco-Prussian War and lived in a garden by a little lake.

"He was an old man with a white beard when I, a boy, tiptoeing in his garden paths, first knew him. He wore, I remember, a velvet skullcap and smoked a large pipe with a white bowl. I can see him yet, moving about at his work, sometimes humming a tune, and bending over with a kind of love to the care of his flowers. Or I think of him sitting at evening in a home-made rustic chair in his own doorway looking out across the garden to the quiet waters of the lake. I never knew any one who

"I think of him sitting at evening in his own doorway look-
ing out across the garden."

could sit so still for so long a time; and as he sat, a great look of peace would come upon his face. He was not married. He wore carpet slippers.

"I never knew, being a boy, why he should be considered mysterious, unless it was that though he had few dishes, few chairs, few dollars, he had books. In that day in the West books were enough to make any man mysterious. And such strange, worn, leather-covered books, all in a foreign language! One, the only one I can remember, was 'Werther' by Goethe.

"He made a poor enough living by selling flowers, aster and pansy plants, and in spring such garden plants as strawberries, tomatoes, cabbages, and peppers. He kept a few hives of bees and a few hens, and trained a grapevine upon the sunny side of his house. He had his flowers in old-fashioned boarded beds with narrow walks between, and in late summer, when the hollyhocks, asters, and zinnias had grown tall, you would see him almost hidden among them, his benignant countenance springing out of a mass of bloom. Well, I am long, Mr. Thorpe, in getting to the point——"

Mr. Thorpe nodded.

"But once the thought of him came to me I

wanted to tell you about him. At first I was somewhat afraid of him; but as time passed I began to like to go into his garden. He exercised a strange fascination that I could not then understand. He would sometimes pick a sprig of geranium, pinch it between his thumb and finger, smell of it himself, and then put it in my buttonhole. He would sometimes speak to me in broken English, but soon lapse into German, not one word of which could I understand. But there was something about his voice— something rich, beautiful, comforting—that made me like to listen to him. And one sentence or motto he said over so many times that one day, quite to his astonishment, I repeated it after him:

"*'Wenn ihr stille bliebt so würde euch geholfen.'*

"When I said it after him, he looked at me keenly.

"*'*Ach!' he said, 'you haf learnt a great t'ing.'

"He paused.

"*'*Do you know what dis means?'

"'No,' said I.

"*'Wenn ihr stille bliebt,* dot means "if you vere qviet"; *so würde euch geholfen,* "so voold help come."'"

As I look back and think now of that old German gardener I am convinced that there *was* some mystery about him; some reason why he left his Fatherland and came to that wild new country and made him a garden to live in. Possibly it was only the ancient mystery of a bruised spirit or a broken heart, possibly it was something more startling, but, be that as it may, one shy boy, tiptoeing in his garden paths, knew that he was a good man, and that he lived at last tranquilly; and that boy was never to forget the motto he had from the old man's lips:

"When you are quiet, help comes."

There isn't really anything more to tell—yet. This is one of the incidents out of life which has not "turned out," but is on its way to the stars. Mr. Thorpe and I parted friends; we have since kept up that friendship. That's the conclusion, if there is any. And how better could any story end than in a friendship?

XII

THE RETURN

In thy home is the truth. Go where thou wilt, to
    Benares or Mathura;
If thy soul is a stranger to thee, the whole world
    is unhomely.
—*From* KABIR, *the Weaver Mystic of Northern India.*

IT was in summer that we came home again.
I shall never forget the little turning beyond
the hill when we came home again. It was
early morning, and there was the smoke of
breakfast fires in many a friendly chimney as
we passed; and I saw the crows lifting and calling from many a dewy field. Dear quiet

"I came newly alive there at the turning, at the sight of the smoke in my own chimney."

Hempfield.   The wide valley, the trees and the hills. *My hills.* I stopped to look at them again, all clear in the morning sun.

"There is old Ransome's barn. . . . There is Darth's tumbledown fence and his Jersey cows. . . . Dold has built a new shed. . . . And there is our own great elm."

It came to me with such a rush of feeling as I cannot describe, how much I loved it all. Dear town; sweet loophole of retreat.

Suddenly, something within me that had long been knotted hard, strained and twisted down in dull, unhappy endurance, began to unknit and loosen away. I came newly alive there at the turning, at the sight of the smoke in my own chimney, and when I next looked up at the hills I could not see them. . . .

I do not intend to relate every step in that recovery. After one stops whirling, he remains for a time still a little dizzy. It seemed to me I wanted to get hold of the firmest, simplest, realest things I could anywhere find. I wanted to be slow and quiet.

"Harriet," I said, "I am not so much in a hurry as I was to write a great book."

She did not answer.

"But one thing I am sure of."

"What is that?" asked Harriet.

"Why, that one can begin living a little book anywhere, at any time."

Most of my notes of that time, I find, are of common work and common, simple people: men driving teams, cutting hay, spraying their orchards, cultivating their corn.

It was, indeed, just at hay-cutting time that I came home again. We had a fine crop in our own meadow; half alfalfa it was, and heavy. I helped at the pitching on until I dripped in the hot sun. I followed the great loads down to the barn. I watched them going in at the gaping doorway. I smelled the cattle in the stanchions below.

I waited for the man on the load to drive down his barbed hayfork, and watched the old horse pull away on the hoisting rope. "Gid-ap there, Moll; gid-ap!"

I heard the squeak of the pulley and saw the great fork full of hay lift upward and shift over the gaping bay.

"Whoa!" cries the man in the dusty mow, and down comes the load upon us.

There are little dusty golden shafts of sunlight coming through holes in the roof; there are startled pigeons in the dim eaves.

The man on the load is bare-headed, bare-armed, bare-chested, and black as an Indian with dust and sunburn.

"Gee, but it's hot," says he, looking down at us.

Walking back to the field with every sense clean, sharp, naked—hungry and thirsty as I had not been before in months—*good* hunger, *honest* thirst—I caught an odour that I did not at first recognise, but that somehow gave me an old thrill. I followed it across a little ravine full of wild blackberry bushes and came to a neglected field-side where there was a world of milkweed in bloom. Do you know the odour of milkweed blossoms on a hot day? Man, if you do not, you have a life yet to live!

"So, it's *you*," said I, "after all these years."

I cannot tell in words what a renewed grip this utterly trivial moment gave me upon the earth. For it bridged suddenly the years backward to my boyhood, and the deep, deep realities I knew then. I recalled vividly a certain hillside covered like this hillside with blossoming milkweeds—where I went with a sword of whittled lath, to slay them where they stood. What blood I shed! What bold thoughts filled me then!

They brought water to the field in a small milk can—with the return from the barn of the empty hayrack. And we all stopped there to drink and look at one another and joke the Polish man on the wagon and laugh at the boy on the hay rake, whose bare legs were too short to reach the release, so that he had to hitch forward from his seat each time he dropped his load.

Drink! How we poured down the blessed cool water there in the hot field. Our Irishman with a fine gesture flung the can on his shoulder and, turning his head to one side, with his mouth twisted awry, drank gloriously, we jeering him.

"It minds me o' the good old days," says he, smacking his lips, "whin hayin' was hayin'."

He drew his bare sweaty arm across his mouth.

"Thim times," said he, "we hayed with a jug —and something in it."

This caused the Pole on the load, who understood this remark perfectly, to laugh immoderately.

"We no get him now," he said.

"That's the true word," responded the Irishman, "or whatever ye do git, it's plain poison."

Next to men at work I love well to see men at rest. I watched to-day one of the boys on a load of hay which he had driven up to the barn. He had to wait a few minutes while another load, then in the barn, was emptied. He was a sturdy young fellow, with great powerful arms and a face burned quite black in the sun; a good worker, as we knew well, for we had pitched to him on the load.

I saw him drop down on the hay while he waited and fling his arms wide there in perfect comfort. I saw him looking up at the sky, half drowsily, at the hens running about in the yard, and presently at the barelegged girl who was now leading the pulley horse. There was a half smile of complete contentment upon his youthful face. It was good to look at him. And when at length the other rack was backed out of the barn and the man in the mow called out, "All right there, come ahead," he sprang up with alacrity, seized the reins and, with legs widely parted, cried out:

"Git up there, Jim; now, Kate——" And he drove gloriously, like a young god, into the great doorway of the barn.

It was by such homely incidents as these— and there were many of them in those first

months after I came home again—it was by
such incidents, and the attempt to realise them
more deeply by setting them down afterward in
my notes, that I seemed to get hold again upon
reality—the true, normal things of the earth.
It is true: we travel in circles and if left to ourselves, return again upon ourselves. . . .

"Harriet," I said, "look there at the cloud on
the horizon. Do you not see the cloud on the
horizon?"

"I see no cloud," said Harriet.

"It is there," I said, "it is the cloud the City
makes. The City is a great invention. It is a
wonderful place, the City. But it is no place
for a man to live."

I knew presently that I was coming truly
alive again by the reviving appetite I had for
everything that happened all about: on my land,
in the country roads, or in the town. For we
may truly test the health of our spirit by the
appetite we have for the common, simple food
of living. And finally one day—this was early
the next spring—I had an adventure with a
peach-tree man which seemed to me to cap my
life with a full recovery, for I could again laugh
at life, as well as look at it.

I had been much pestered that spring with interruptions of all kinds. It is a curious subject upon which I have done some reflecting—this matter of interruptions. Although I pretend to be much provoked and disgusted with interruptions, I have a kind of fondness for them. (This is a secret.) Often and often when I have set myself to a hard task—grim-jawed, determined—I can't prevent a little imp somewhere in the back of my mind jumping up and down and literally yelping for some kind of an interruption, anything—a man coming down the lane, or the postman, or a voice from the doorway, "Telephone, David."

And at the very moment I feel sternest toward all interrupters I know in my heart that I like nothing better in this world than to pounce upon some neighbour who is contentedly at work and surprise, and steal his secret of contentment. One gets little from an idle man; much from a busy, happy man; and how can one get to a busy, happy man, I'd like to know, without interrupting him?

Nevertheless, I do like variety in interrupters, and the Peach-Tree Man I speak of was the third or fourth nursery-stock salesman who had come smiling down my lane within two weeks. When I saw him with his picture book under one arm, and a couple of sample peach trees, their roots wonderfully wrapped in burlap, under the other, I hastily scrabbled around in my mind for just the phrase which would send him back up the hill—not exactly bleeding or badly hurt, but finished! I was getting my bees out of winter quarters and was very busy. It is one of the disadvantages of the farmer that his office is all outdoors; there is no polite stenographer at the gate to say, "I'm sorry, but Mr. Grayson is engaged."

But this salesman was a downright good one. I feel certain he must have been graduated somewhere with the degree of D.P.P. (Doctor of Practical Psychology). For he caught me while I was figuratively reaching for my gun, and there I was, looking at his wonderful coloured pictures of the rosiest, yellowest, biggest peaches ever grown this side the Garden of Eden; I was hearing his dulcet explanations of how his trees were selected and budded and pruned and root-pruned; and I could see for myself, as he deftly turned over his sample, how well his great, reliable, sincere, honest, earnest, patriotic, one-hundred-per-cent-American company packed its trees for shipment.

Oh, he was a smart one! I resisted with all my might, looked cold and distant, was sententious in my utterances, even two or three times made as if to return to my work, but I felt myself slipping, slipping.

I had a wild idea of opening one of the hives near at hand—casually and absent-mindedly as it were—and letting come what would. The thought of that agent retreating up the hill and trying to be dignified with twenty angry honey-bees at each ear was a picture of some attraction.

Suddenly a great idea recurred to me. It had served me once before; and it has been good for more than one crisis since. It is also now in use, with great success, by several of my neighbours. It is a simple and delightful idea; and I give it here free to all the world, without patent, trade-mark, or copyright.

"Excuse me," I said to the Peach-Tree Man, "excuse me for just a moment. I've got something I want to show you."

He let go without enthusiasm, and I went to the house and came back with a copy of my last book. (A cake of honey or a bushel of potatoes will do as well.)

I opened my book there before the somewhat

perplexed Peach-Tree Man and told him with what care I had selected and budded the ideas I put into it, how afterward I had both pruned and root-pruned them.

"And you will see finally," I said, talking fast, "how perfectly my company has covered and packed my production so that it won't dry out, or die—so, in fact, that it will start an interesting growth in any soil whatsoever in which it is planted, and finally produce the most beautiful, gorgeous, delicious fruit known to man."

I enlarged upon the profit he would secure if he took my book at only a dollar and seventy-five cents, treated it well, fertilised and cultivated it; and what happiness he would presently have at the harvest.

"And," said I when I was beginning to get out of breath, "it will last long and bear well after every peach tree in your packet has been planted, grown, harvested, and died."

I shall not soon forget the look of amazement that slowly grew in his eye; amazement and irritation. It was something plainly unexpected and wholly new to him—this interruption of the interrupter. (That's my slogan: "Interrupt the interrupter.")

"Say, mister," said he, "I don't want to buy books.   I'm sellin' trees."

"Well, mister," I responded, "I don't want to buy trees.   I'm selling books."

For once in his life this excellent Peach-Tree Man, D.P.P., was plainly dazed and did not know what to say.   We looked at each other solemnly a moment—and rather helplessly, too, and then suddenly we both began to laugh— irresistibly.

As soon as I could get a chance I said to him:

"Did you ever hear of the Roman augurs?"

"I've heard of carpenters' augers," said he doubtfully, "and ship's augers, but I ain't never, zi know of, heard of Roman augers."

"Well," said I, "they were an interesting lot. They were a kind of fortune-teller, you know, clairvoyants——"

"Them fakers," said the cheerful Peach-Tree Man.

"Exactly," said I.

"And they called 'em augurs?"

"In Rome, yes. . . . Well, they got so they could fool the people perfectly—but of course they couldn't fool one another.   You'll under-stand that."

"Sure—I know—sure."

"So it was said that when one augur met another in Rome he couldn't help winking at him."

I stopped a moment and waited. The Peach-Tree Man turned this curious and unexpected bit of historical information over in his mind—I could literally see him turning it! But I awaited the exact moment when he should look up with puzzled understanding.

I was on tenterhooks, I can tell you, but at last it came; and then and not till then, exactly at the right instant, I winked at him solemnly. I was sure enough of him as a Yankee, a trader, and a D.P.P. to feel that he would not miss the point.

He did not. The smile which had begun to come disappeared, and, with a face as solemn as my own, he also winked.

This was again followed by a somewhat awkward pause. There just didn't seem anything more to be said—by augurs who completely understood each other. It was the Peach-Tree Man who broke the silence.

"Good-morning, mister," said he in a kind of husky voice, and before I could respond he hurried up the hill and turned into the town road.

"Good-by, augur," I called after him, but he did not look around.

A few minutes later my neighbour B——came along and said to me that he had just met a man coming out of my lane with something the matter with him, terribly red in the face. Mad? What had I done to him?

With that I walked slowly up the hill and came to the road, and there on a little embankment sat my Peach-Tree Man. He seemed to be in pain.

"What's the trouble?" I asked.

"Mister," said he, "I ain't laughed so much in a dog's life. Say, where did you get that line of talk? That's a dang good one."

With that his face sobered down suddenly and, although there were tears in his eyes, he winked at me solemnly and I as solemnly returned it. Then he took my arm and said:

"See here, mister, you an' me ought not to part this way. You and me ought to trade."

I said he was a good one!

"Look here," he continued, "I'll buy your book, if you'll buy some o' my trees. I'd just like to see what a feller like you would put in a book."

"And I," said I, "would like to see how near your peaches come to your pictures."

And so, on the spot, we settled it.   I took the trees and he took my book.

"Come back in three or four years," I said to him, "and tell me how you like my book and I'll tell you how I like your peaches."

"You bet," said he, "you bet—I'll come back before that."

(I'll bet he will too!)

So he went off up the road with my book close clasped under his arm along with his gorgeous peach-tree catalogue.

"Harriet," said I when I got back to the house, "now I am prepared for anything. Bring on your wonders."

So I am at home again, and think it will take an earthquake in addition to a war to get me away again.   Here I live.   After wandering, this valley is my home, this very hillside, these green acres.   Here all about me are friends I love; friends living and friends in old books. This is my progress, the process of the seasons; this my reward, the product of the earth and the work of my own hand and brain.   I

want no other.   Here may I be quiet, and think
and love and work.   Here, when I lift up my
eyes, I can see the fire smouldering in the
Bush; I can hear from the clouds a Voice.

THE END,